To:

_____

From:

_____

Date:

_____

peace, be still

180 Quiet-Time
Prayers for
Teen *Girls*

JANICE THOMPSON

BARBOUR
PUBLISHING

Peace, Be Still!

Sweet girl! Did you realize that God created you—
yes, you!—to live in peace? It's true! In spite of the
craziness, the busyness, the chaotic life you lead;
in spite of your family stuff, your schoolwork, and
more, it's still possible. In the middle of the chaos, in
the very center of the storms, as you face Goliath-
sized problems, you can find true and lasting peace
when you turn to Jesus.

God's call to peace requires *one* very special
thing of you—that you draw near to Him. It's not easy
with everything swirling around you. But there, in
that quiet place, He will give you the tools you need
to shake off that craziness and replace it with His
supernatural peace.

Are you ready to be changed from the inside
out? Great! Use the prayers in this little book as a
guide as you enter His presence. They can jump-
start your peace journey, no matter what you're
walking through.

Only in Your Presence

*"I have told you these things so you may have peace
in Me. In the world you will have much trouble.
But take hope! I have power over the world!"*

JOHN 16:33 NLV

I need peace, Jesus! This world is a whirling, swirling mess most of the time, and that's without all the school craziness! (Do we even have to go there?) I don't know if I'm coming or going, if I'm up or I'm down. There are days when I feel like I can't even catch my breath.

On those days, I need Your true and lasting peace more than ever. Please send it like a blanket. Surround me with Your quietness, Your calm. Still my heart when it's thump-thump-thumping out of control. I need a reminder that You can bring calm in the middle of the hurricane!

You are right there, in the eye of the storms that come my way, even the ones that scare me to death! The winds are howling, but I will step into that peaceful center to spend time with You. Once I'm there, I will find peace. Meet me there, I pray. Amen.

My Burden Is Light

*If you are tired from carrying heavy burdens,
come to me and I will give you rest. Take the yoke
I give you. Put it on your shoulders and learn from me.
I am gentle and humble, and you will find rest. This
yoke is easy to bear, and this burden is light.*

MATTHEW 11:28 — 30 CEV

Jesus, I'm struggling to hold it all! These burdens feel like boulders placed on my shoulders. They're weighing me down. I can hardly stand up straight! Why do I even try? I want to toss them, to ditch them once and for all.

I'm so happy Your Word says I can come to You with those boulder-like burdens. You will give me rest. You swap out a heavy burden for a soft, fluffy pillow filled with weightless feathers. Ahh!

I toss that pillow in the air, easy-breezy, and watch the evening sun shimmer off it as I catch it in my arms again. Thank You for doing the heavy lifting so I don't have to. I love this swap, Father! Your yoke really is easy. And those burdens? They're featherlight. Amen.

I Will Be Still

*"Be still, and know that I am God! I will
be honored by every nation. I will be
honored throughout the world."*

PSALM 46:10 NLT

I love how my dog stares up at me with a look of pure love, Jesus! Oh, those big brown eyes! I melt every time! My pup knows he can trust me because I've never shown him anything but love. Okay, so I spoil him a little, but that's normal, right? He knows I'll give him every good thing, probably more than he needs. He cuddles at my side or curls up at my feet, content to simply be with me. My presence is enough for him. He feels comfortable, safe, and loved. And he is! I adore him.

This is how I feel when I'm with You, Lord! You're the kindest Master of all. You have the best treats—joy, peace, loving-kindness. I want to curl up at Your feet, content in the fact that You simply want to be with me. I will be still in Your presence and enjoy Your goodness, Your kindness, Your vast love for me. Why would I ever want for another when I have You, the Lover of my soul? Amen.

In Every Way

*May the Lord of peace give you His peace
at all times. The Lord be with you all.*

2 THESSALONIANS 3:16 NLV

I'm only in my teens, but I feel like I've already messed up so many times, Jesus. (Hey, I guess I'm not telling You anything You don't already know!) Still, You were right there, watching every dumb move I made, whispering, *"Maybe that's not such a great idea, kiddo."* I didn't always pay attention, and I'm sorry!

I feel bad about so many mistakes. I took many wrong paths. They led me down dark roads into shadowy forests, where I faced battles I didn't know were coming.

But You? You've been so awesome to pick me up, dust me off, and put me on the right road once again, Lord! You didn't make me feel like a loser for going the wrong way. You just said, *"I love you anyway,"* and proved it with Your actions.

Here's a confession: When I'm on the wrong road, I usually know it. It doesn't take me long to figure out that my peace is gone when I'm headed the wrong way. That's why I want to keep my hand in Yours, Jesus. You keep me safe, and I'm so grateful. Amen.

The Important Things

He said to them, "Come away from the people. Be by yourselves and rest." There were many people coming and going. They had had no time even to eat.

MARK 6:31 NLV

There are so many things in my life that are important to me, Jesus: my family, school stuff, my friends, our home, my talents, my future. . .all these made the "important things" list, along with many, many more.

Sometimes I'm so caught up with all the goodies in my world that I forget some of the most important things of all. Maybe that's because they're not really "things." You want me to remember to eat well, take care of myself, and rest. I don't always do that, especially when things are crazy with my schedule. And sometimes I pay a price for ignoring them.

Thank You for reminding me that the things in my life are important, but nothing is as important as an obedient heart that follows hard after You. Today I give You the most important "thing" of all. . .my heart. Amen.

Pursued by Your Goodness

*For sure, You will give me goodness and loving-
kindness all the days of my life. Then I will
live with You in Your house forever.*

PSALM 23:6 NLV

I've always been a little weirded out by the story of Hosea,
Jesus. I mean, You told him to choose a prostitute for a wife.
Um. . . But I love the part about how he refused to give up on
her, even when she kept going back to other men. That part
was cool. Hosea chased her down over and over and won her
heart. She eventually came back home. She learned the true
message of this verse: "For sure, You will give me goodness
and loving-kindness all the days of my life. Then I will live
with You in Your house forever."

I get it, Lord! Their story is a beautiful picture of how You
love us! You love us so gently and beautifully that we can't
help but come back home to hang out with You.

I'm dazzled by Your love, and I'm blown away when You
pursue me, even when I wander off and chase other "loves."
Your goodness and unfailing love will continue to follow me
until the day I leave this earth to go to heaven, where I'll spend
eternity with You. Thank You, thank You! Amen.

I Won't Trust Myself

*Trust in the L<small>ORD</small> with all your heart, and do
not lean on your own understanding.*

PROVERBS 3:5 ESV

I'm learning, Jesus! I can place my trust in You and nobody else. Man, have I tried trusting people. Talk about an epic fail! The stories I could tell!

Now that I've tasted and seen Your goodness, Your grace, and Your mercy, I'm hooked on You and You alone. You promise to stick with me, and I know You will. I feel Your love. Who else cares like You? No one! You make it easy to love You.

Because I feel loved, I can walk in peace from day to day. I don't have to wonder if You're going to give up on me. I know You won't! I can know for sure that You will never leave me or abandon me. You never have, and You never will.

My hands want to reach for the sky! I want to worship You not just today but all the days of my life! I place my trust in You alone. Amen.

A Present Help

God is our safe place and our strength.
He is always our help when we are in trouble.

PSALM 46:1 NLV

Lord, You saw me frozen in place like the paralyzed man in the Bible. I was locked in fear. I couldn't take a step forward or backward. It gave me such hope when You said, "Rise up and walk!" And when I saw the love pouring from Your eyes, Jesus, I truly believed I could.

So I did! I rose from my sleep. I rose from my pain. I rose from the past, the icky decisions I'd made, the bad crowd I'd hung out with. And I felt a smile tug at the corners of my lips for the first time in years—not because of anything I had done but because of Your amazing love. It made me brave! It brought me peace. It gave me strength.

Lord, You truly are my help when I'm in trouble. You dive headfirst into my situation, no matter how complicated, no matter how messy. With so much love, You say, "You can do this, girl. With My help, you can." And in that moment, I know You are right! I put my hand in Yours today, Lord. I know You'll keep me safe. Amen.

Victory through Faith

Every child of God can defeat the world,
and our faith is what gives us this victory.

1 JOHN 5:4 CEV

Jesus, sometimes I don't see myself as a winner. I look at my track record and think *Loser!* not *Winner*. (Just keeping it real. I have a lousy battle record.) Sometimes I even give up before the fight begins. That's how defeated I feel. (Hey, I told You I was keeping it real!)

I'm so glad to hear that You *always* win. There's never been a battle in the history of, well, *ever* that You've lost. What a track record, Lord! You're a victor every single time. Wow! No one else can say that, not even the strongest warrior on the planet.

So I put my trust in You! With You on my team, I can be victorious in every battle I face, whether I'm feeling like a winner or not. "Winning" might not look the way I think it should, but You'll continue to surprise me with new and exciting ways to view my victories.

Let's do this, Lord! I'm ready to hit the battlefield with Your hand in mine and peace leading the way! Amen.

Your Path Brings Peace

Keep alert. Be firm in your faith.
Stay brave and strong.

1 CORINTHIANS 16:13 CEV

Follow the Leader seemed like a fun game when I was a little kid, as long as I got to be the leader. (Hey, what can I say? I've always had great leadership abilities!)

Okay, okay. . .I just like to boss people around, truth be told, but You already know that, Lord. It's not as easy to follow, but I'm working on it, especially when it comes to following You. You make following fun.

Some of my friends have the opposite problem. They're followers, not leaders. I cringe when I watch them, because they don't always follow the right people. They end up headed straight for a ditch!

I will give up my need to always lead, Father. Instead, I will point my heart toward You and follow hard and fast after You, no one else. You lead me down a beautiful path toward meadows where I can rest. Ahh! Your path brings peace, so I choose Your way. Amen.

Dirty Hearts and Dishes

But we know that God accepts only those who have faith in Jesus Christ. No one can please God by simply obeying the Law. So we put our faith in Christ Jesus, and God accepted us because of our faith.

GALATIANS 2:16 CEV

I've washed a lot of dishes, and one thing always bugs me—when I spend time scrubbing something, but it still has spots when I'm done. Sometimes I don't notice until I pull a dish from the cupboard. But I'm always grossed out when I see a dirty streak running down the center of the plate. Ugh.

Sometimes I feel like my heart is like that plate. I've allowed You to wash clean certain areas, but I've held back others because of fear or pain. Or maybe I think I've allowed You to finish the job when in reality I've held something back without even realizing it. I usually figure it out when I'm having an argument with a friend. Or my mom. Out it all comes in all its dirty glory. Ick! How embarrassing.

Today I ask You to wash me clean from head to toe, heart to mind. I don't want any stains to stick around after Your great heart wash, Jesus! I can only walk in total peace when I've allowed You to do a thorough cleaning! Amen.

Faith Encourages Actions

Because Noah had faith, he built a large boat for his family. God told him what was going to happen. His faith made him hear God speak and he obeyed. His family was saved from death because he built the boat. In this way, Noah showed the world how sinful it was. Noah became right with God because of his faith in God.

HEBREWS 11:7 NLV

Going on a trip is so much fun, Lord. Getting ready for the trip is too! Imagining the places we will go, the things we will do, the cool experiences we will have. Preparing for the adventure is half the fun!

In some ways, my life is like that. When I walk with You—and trust You fully with my future—I get so excited about what's coming! I'm totally at peace because I know the adventures in front of me are safely mapped out, part of Your plan.

I want to be like Noah when it comes to life's great adventures. Even when I can't see with my eyes, give me the courage to act. Even if others make fun of me, give me peace about the adventure ahead. And give me the necessary tools to build whatever needs building—in my heart, my mind, my soul—so that I'm fully prepared when the time is right. Amen.

Slow Down. . .and Dine!

Jesus replied: I am the bread that gives life!
No one who comes to me will ever be hungry.
No one who has faith in me will ever be thirsty.

JOHN 6:35 CEV

My life is crazy busy, Jesus! I run here, there, and everywhere . . .always in a hurry. I feel like I'm so rushed that I don't have the time to slow down and truly enjoy where I am most of the time.

Will life be this fast when I'm grown up? Will I always feel so rushed? So busy? Why am I always longing for that next big thing? Why am I always thirsting after the thrill of the next grand adventure?

Thank You for the reminder that I don't need to hunger and thirst after anything but You. There's no frantic pace with You either, Lord. Only peace. Sweet, calming peace. No chasing after this or that. No rushing around. Whew! You are the Bread of Life. When I take the time to come to You, the clock stops. You feed me and satisfy my every need. Slowing down will bring me peace. I need that! Amen.

A Fixed Mind

*"The Lord gives perfect peace
to those whose faith is firm."*

ISAIAH 26:3 CEV

I'm so stressed out today, Lord! Ugh! I don't like the way this feels. I know I should give these problems to You, but sometimes I'm hanging on to them so tightly that it's hard to unwind my fingers. I feel like You have to pry them out of my hands.

Help me let go, I pray! Give me faith to believe You're bigger than what I'm facing right now. I don't need much faith. . .just a tiny mustard seed's worth. Show me how to keep my mind hyperfocused on You, not the problems. They're swarming around me so fast—like bees buzzing around my head. Sometimes it's hard to notice anything else. I honestly feel lost in a daze of confusion when things get like this. Help!

I'm sorry for the times I've allowed myself to get caught up in the drama of chaotic circumstances, Father. I want to keep my mind on You. Solid. Immovable. You. Only there will I find the peace to make all the right choices. Help me, I pray! Amen.

Worked to the Bone

*It is useless to get up early and stay up
late in order to earn a living. God takes care
of his own, even while they sleep.*

PSALM 127:2 CEV

I get so tired sometimes, Lord. I feel like I have no strength at all. Even when there's nothing physically wrong with me, sometimes I feel like there is because I can't seem to move at the same pace as before. I wonder if others feel as zapped as I do. They keep going, going, going, like Energizer Bunnies.

I just can't. I'm done. There's no moving forward. I'm just too tired.

Then You sweep in and energize me with Your love. You give me strength for the journey when I need it most. You bring peace, strength, energy, joy, resilience. All these things are Your free gifts to me just for spending time with You.

And then I realize that's what I've been missing! I've been so busy working that I forgot to take time with You. No wonder my life is so out of balance, so off-kilter! Thank You for the reminder that the greater work is to just be with You. Amen.

How Abundant Your Goodness!

*How great is the goodness you have stored
up for those who fear you. You lavish it
on those who come to you for protection,
blessing them before the watching world.*

PSALM 31:19 NLT

Everything else seems dull when I compare it to Your glory and grace, Jesus! Monstrous problems that looked like they might swallow me in the night are revealed as what they are—illusions. Shadows. Your goodness overwhelms them in a hurry! Wow!

Nothing compares to You, Lord. If I took all the coolest people I've ever known in my life and lined them up next to each other, their worth combined wouldn't even come close to who You are. You are my great Redeemer. My Forgiver. My hope. You're the One who can bring peace when no one else can. No one I know can bring real change to my life. But You, Lord? You've done all of that and more. And You have done it all out of Your great love for me. What peace, to rest in Your goodness. I'm Your grateful daughter.

Amen.

A Prayer for a Friend

When I am afraid, I will trust in You. I praise the
Word of God. I have put my trust in God. I will
not be afraid. What can only a man do to me?

PSALM 56:3–4 NLV

I'm scared, Lord. I'm worried something bad will happen to someone I love. My friend is in a tough place and isn't strong right now. In fact, she seems to be falling apart at the seams! Nothing I say seems to make a difference. She doesn't seem to hear me or listen to my advice. There's nothing I can do but pray.

That's why I've come to You today, Lord, to let You know how much she needs You! Heal her. . .please! Touch her heart. Bring peace. Calm things down in a hurry. Show her the way to break free once and for all!

And when You're done with all of that, would You touch my heart too? I don't want to waste any time worrying when I could be encouraging her. Show me how to be the best sort of friend, not one who makes things worse, but one who loves her through this. I will trust You with my friend, Lord. Amen.

Light as a Feather

"Do not fear, for I am with you. Do not be afraid, for I am your God. I will give you strength, and for sure I will help you. Yes, I will hold you up with My right hand that is right and good."

ISAIAH 41:10 NLV

Today I watched some birds land on the fence and then take off again, headed to a nearby bush. They didn't stay there for long. A few seconds later, they were on their way to the next yard, where they landed on the branch of a magnolia tree. Those tiny creatures seemed to float across the air, weightless and carefree, like ripples on the afternoon breeze.

That's how I feel when I place my trust in You, Lord! I'm so light, so carefree, that I move easily from one situation to the next. Freedom is a gift from You.

I want to live like this, Lord! Not weighed down by the cares of life but light as a feather! Only You can perform this kind of miracle, but I'm believing for it, in spite of the weight of the circumstances I face. Lift me up, Lord, far above the circumstances, and teach me how to soar! Amen.

Healing through Confession

Tell your sins to each other. And pray for each
other so you may be healed. The prayer from the
heart of a man right with God has much power.

JAMES 5:16 NLV

It's so much easier to hold it all inside, Jesus. Seriously! I
usually keep the bad things I've done to myself. It's nobody's
business. But I know from experience that confession really
is good for the soul. Opening up? Sharing? It's so hard, but
You say it's important to bring healing and true peace.

I'm so glad You've placed friends and loved ones in my life
whom I can trust. When I need broad shoulders to lean on, I
can count on those You've sent to walk alongside me.

I'm also learning that I can always run to You, Lord. When
my heart feels as heavy as lead, when I'm feeling guilty or
aching with pain, You say, *"Bring it to Me, girl!"* And when I
need to confess something, You listen as my patient Father,
ready to forgive me every single time. How loving You are!
How grateful I am.

So I come today, ready to share my heart. I know You'll use
this time to bring healing. Amen.

You Pour Out Your Great Love

*Hope never makes us ashamed because the
love of God has come into our hearts through
the Holy Spirit Who was given to us.*

ROMANS 5:5 NLV

"He loves me, he loves me not."

I remember yanking petals from a flower as I spoke those words as a little girl. I've had lots of crushes, Jesus! That boy in my science class in third grade? Yeah, that didn't last. He loved me not. But You? I will never have to wonder about Your love! It brings peace to my heart when I remember that You will love me all my days, good and bad.

"He loves me!" What joy!

I've never known the kind of love You pour out on me, Lord! It's so rich with forgiveness, and it bubbles over with mercy and grace. When I rest in this love of Yours, I'm changed from the inside out! I don't have to worry about anything I've done (or not done). I can simply "be" in Your presence. Whew! That's a huge relief. Thanks so much for pouring out Your love! Amen.

A Loving Shepherd

Know that the Lord, he is God! It is he
who made us, and we are his; we are his
people, and the sheep of his pasture.

PSALM 100:3 ESV

You are a good shepherd, Lord, *the* Good Shepherd. You look after the sheep in Your pasture with tenderness and love. No wolf or lion can come near as long as You stand guard as Protector! I can trust You, Lord, even when I'm feeling scared and alone. You are right there, guarding, protecting, and giving me peace. I know that no enemy can come near as long as You're on the job. They can try, sure. But none of them can penetrate Your invisible barrier. I'm safe with You!

Best of all, You tell me that I belong to You! I'm in the right pasture. You want me. You fought hard to win me. So why would I ever wander from the Shepherd who loves me more than anyone else possibly could? No, I'll stay put, Jesus, safe in Your care.

Thank You, my Good Shepherd. Amen.

My Creator Is Re-creating Me!

*And I praise you because of the wonderful
way you created me. Everything you do is
marvelous! Of this I have no doubt.*

PSALM 139:14 CEV

With just a word, You created the heavens and the earth, Lord. You took nothing—absolutely nothing—and spun whole worlds into existence. You hung the stars, the sun, and the moon in place. Then You formed the earth—that magnificent blue ball—and filled it with living, breathing things. . . including me! Wow! And boy, did You take Your time with me. Your Word says that I am fearfully and wonderfully made, every cell, every freckle, every detail.

When I think of all You can do, when I remember all You've already done, it reminds me that You are able to re-create me. You can take the messes I've made and breathe new life into them. You can take this dried-up, withered heart and—just as the Spirit hovered over the waters at creation—spring it to life once again, from death to an amazing life.

You're the most amazing Creator of all, Lord, and I'm so grateful You're re-creating me! Amen.

I Will Look to You

Let us keep looking to Jesus. Our faith comes from Him and He is the One Who makes it perfect. He did not give up when He had to suffer shame and die on a cross. He knew of the joy that would be His later. Now He is sitting at the right side of God.

HEBREWS 12:2 NLV

My life is in Your hands, Jesus, not my own! I try to make things happen. . .oh boy, do I try! But none of my slick moves compare with Yours! With just a word, You can change everything. You *have* changed everything. I'm really peaceful when I take my hands off the reins, because I know I can trust You to guide me wherever I need to go.

I love this verse so much! "He is the One Who makes it perfect." That's why I'm comfortable handing the reins to You—because You really do make all things perfect. I've seen it thousands of times. I toss the puzzle pieces of my life into the air, they land all over the place, and You somehow, miraculously, put them together in a lovely picture. (How do You do that, anyway?!) Why would I look to anyone but You? I won't, Lord! My eyes are staying on You. Amen.

Too Spicy to Handle!

"Blessed are the peacemakers,
for they shall be called sons of God."

MATTHEW 5:9 ESV

I've been thinking about that time my mom put too much spice in a pot of chili she was making. It was too hot to handle, for sure. It did a number on my mouth. . .and my stomach. Ugh.

That's how I feel about some of the people in my world sometimes, Jesus! They're just too much to take, way too hot to handle! They're too spicy for me! They leave me in pain. They overwhelm me and try to steal my peace.

I need Your help to deal with them the right way, Jesus. I can only take them in small doses. Too much and. . .yowza! And yet, they keep showing up, and I let them in to steal my time, my energy, and my peace.

It's time to change all of that, but I can't do it alone. Help me navigate these awkward relationships, I pray. Give me wisdom to know when to take a bite of that spicy chili. . .and when not to. Amen.

It's Only Possible with You, Lord

But he said, "What is impossible with man is possible with God."

LUKE 18:27 ESV

Is there an answer to the world's problems, Lord? Everything's such a mess! No one gets along. People get so worked up about everything. Problems are everywhere. When I turn on the news, I want to cry. And finding solutions? It seems impossible, especially when I try to do it the world's way.

I'm learning, Jesus! You're the only solution to the problem. You are the One who can fix the brokenness. You're the only One who can bring real change, the One who brings hope to the hopeless. Only You, Lord. Nobody else!

I won't look to anything or anyone else but You, Lord. Answers aren't found in this world. They're not located inside of me or in the voice of a trusted friend, even though You sometimes use my friends to speak to me. I find answers in You and Your Word.

With You, all things are possible. With the world? Not so much. Amen.

Rivers of Living Water

"Anyone who believes in me may come and drink! For the Scriptures declare, 'Rivers of living water will flow from his heart.'"

JOHN 7:38 NLT

Jesus, sometimes I think about what must be going on in heaven right now while I am still here on earth. Are You up there building mansions as we speak? Are You gathering the great musicians who've already passed away and organizing a heavenly choir? Are You taking care of my loved ones who went on ahead of me?

It boggles my mind to think about how amazing heaven must be! How brilliant! How shiny! And when I think of the icky situations I'm facing here on earth, they seem like nothing when I compare them to eternity. There is no problem so great that a little heavenly perspective will not set it right again.

Until I see it all face-to-face, thank You for providing rivers of living water for me to enjoy—right here, right now. Whenever I feel my peace fading, I drink from the stream that never runs dry, and I am revived! How grateful I am! Amen.

The Breeze of Your Spirit

*There is no fear in love, but perfect love casts
out fear. For fear has to do with punishment,
and whoever fears has not been perfected in love.*

1 JOHN 4:18 ESV

Outside my window, the leaves blow briskly by. They are
caught up in a breeze that carries them from our yard to the
lot next door. Those colorful leaves are not in charge. They
are just travelers, moving along as they are led by the breeze.

Sometimes I feel like those leaves, Jesus! Circumstances
happen, and they carry me to places I did not mean to go. As
I'm being whipped around by that unfamiliar wind, I struggle with fear. Where will I land? Will I be okay? Can I trust
the process?

Then I'm reminded that You are in the breeze. I can trust
You to carry me wherever I need to go. I can be totally at
peace when I trust You. You have great plans for my life. Your
perfect love can cast out fear, even when I'm not sure where
I'm headed next. What peace, to trust in You even when I
can't see what's ahead. Today, I choose to move by the wind
of Your Spirit, Lord! Amen.

I Will Keep Pushing Through

Fight the good fight of faith. Take hold of the life that lasts forever. You were chosen to receive it. You have spoken well about this life in front of many people.

1 TIMOTHY 6:12 NLV

There are certain things in my life I'm sure I can't do without, Jesus. If I'm being honest, I'd have to say I'm addicted to many of them. Oops!

For sure, some of these addictions are unhealthy. They mess up my peace because they steal so much from me. They hold my time, health, and joy hostage. What's more, these addictions are starting to worry my friends. They're concerned about me.

So am I, Jesus! I don't like to admit it, but I am a little worried. I don't want to live addicted to anything but You. Set me free from the things that hold me hostage, please! Give me the courage to say no to the things that I want if they are not Your best for me, Lord. I'll keep powering through, fighting the good fight of faith as I try to let go of the things You never meant for me to hold on to. Instead, I'll only hold on to You, Jesus! Amen.

No Waves

If you do not have wisdom, ask God for it. He is always ready to give it to you and will never say you are wrong for asking. You must have faith as you ask Him. You must not doubt. Anyone who doubts is like a wave which is pushed around by the sea. Such a man will get nothing from the Lord. The man who has two ways of thinking changes in everything he does.

JAMES 1:5–8 NLV

I'm remembering an adventure I went on with my family when I was just a little kid, Jesus. We were floating down the river in our inner tubes when I flipped out of mine and the tube went floating downstream, away from me. The current was in control! Up and down it bobbed with every wave, until at last someone was able to catch it. Whew!

I don't want to be like that inner tube. I don't want every strong wind to toss me this way or that. I want to be steady in You. If I can hang tight with You, I'll be safe!

I'm so grateful You dove into the river and caught me, even when I was floating away in my sinful state! You rescued me and saved me from destruction, Jesus. Thank You so much for being the best lifeguard ever! Amen.

Early in the Morning

*Each morning let me learn more about your
love because I trust you. I come to you in
prayer, asking for your guidance.*

PSALM 143:8 CEV

You speak to me at all times of day, Jesus. But there's something so special about the early morning hours when I'm just waking up. Before my mind is cluttered with the craziness of the day, I can lean in close to hear Your voice more clearly.

In those moments, when I'm still under the covers, I'm overwhelmed by Your love and faithfulness. In that peaceful place, everything seems fresh, new, and possible. I love those special morning moments with You! I can start my day at peace, Jesus, because I hear from You first thing. You guide me in the right direction, a holy GPS, giving instructions I didn't even know I needed!

I know You want to hear from me first thing too. So I will pour out my heart in the morning hours and give You the best part of my day. Thank You for meeting me there. And thank You for the peace that is beyond understanding as I face each new precious day. What a gift! Amen.

Hidden in My Heart

I have hidden your word in my heart
that I might not sin against you.

PSALM 119:11 NIV

Peek-a-boo! I've played that game so many times with the little kids I know. Eyes covered, I pull my hands away and giggle with delight as "peek-a-boo!" rings out. What fun! And how surprised they always seem to see me once again!

There's something so cool about being surprised. It never goes away no matter how old I get. That's how I feel about spending time in Your Word, Jesus. Peek-a-boo! There's a verse I never noticed before. Oh look! There's another one, perfect for a hard situation I'm facing. Peek-a-boo! Exactly what I needed to face that icky thing I'm going through with a frenemy. To think, that verse was there all along, just waiting for me. Wow!

I'm so grateful for that life-giving Word that You've hidden deep in my heart. It always delights and surprises me and at just the right time too! There are always adventures when I see Your Word as a box filled with heavenly jewels! Amen.

All I Could Need and More

*I pray that because of the riches of His shining-greatness,
He will make you strong with power in your hearts
through the Holy Spirit. I pray that Christ may live in your
hearts by faith. I pray that you will be filled with love.*
EPHESIANS 3:16–17 NLV

Jesus, sometimes I look at all the areas where I fall short, where I'm lacking talent or skill, and I think, *There's just no way.* . . . I'll never be able to do what needs to be done. No way! I won't finish the school project on time. I won't have a good-paying job like I want to have. I start to panic, thinking about all the things that won't happen.

Then I remember that You own the cattle on a thousand hills. You have access to every available resource, even those things I can't see with my eyes. So I trust You, Lord. I'll calm down and put my faith in the One who owns it all. And I'll remind myself that what I can't accomplish on my own is Yours to deal with. You see my lack. You see my schedule. You see my everything. . .and You're already on the job, making sure I have all I need and more to reach the goal.

I'm so grateful for Your provision, Father! Amen.

A Way Out

*The temptations in your life are no different from
what others experience. And God is faithful.
He will not allow the temptation to be more than
you can stand. When you are tempted, he will
show you a way out so that you can endure.*

1 CORINTHIANS 10:13 NLT

I want it. I *really* want it. But I know if I have it—and I could grab it with my bare hands right at this very moment—I'll regret it. Poor decisions never lead to peace in the end. So I'm asking for Your help, Lord. You can get rid of my desires for the wrong things. You can lean down and whisper these words in my ear: *"That's not a good idea."*

I'm asking You to do that—even with the things I really, really want. If they're not Your best for me, then give me the courage to say no, Lord. On the other side of my "No" is a *"Job well done!"* from You. That's worth a lot more to me than giving in, for sure! And I know for a fact that Your peace is more important than satisfying my temporary longings. Your peace lasts forever. Those temptations? They're fleeting. So I'll fight the temptation—and with Your help, I will overcome. Amen.

Oh, the Greatness of Your Love!

*And may you have the power to understand, as all
God's people should, how wide, how long, how high,
and how deep his love is. May you experience the
love of Christ, though it is too great to understand
fully. Then you will be made complete with all the
fullness of life and power that comes from God.*

EPHESIANS 3:18–19 NLT

I sense it every day, Jesus! The greatness of Your amazing love sweeps over me, changing me with Your goodness. Even when I feel like I don't deserve it, You pour it out like water from a faucet, a beautiful flow to clean up even the grimiest parts of me, the bits I want to hide from everyone.

I could never hide from You, Jesus! You have X-ray vision, anyway. I'm safe in Your care, and I'm reminded of just how deep Your love is—how wide, how long, how high. When I'm there, hanging out with You, nothing else matters. I don't try to make sense of it, to overthink it. Instead, I soak in it, like a dry sponge getting wet for the first time. Your touch changes everything.

Thank You, Jesus! You complete me with Your amazing love. It's the missing ingredient, the hole filler, the power giver, the light for my path. Show me how to love like You do so that others can have this same life-changing peace. Amen.

Live at Peace

Do all that you can to live in peace with everyone.

ROMANS 12:18 NLT

They don't make it easy, Lord. There are people in my life—You know the ones—who grate on my nerves because they always seem to stir up problems. They're *not* easy to get along with. Just the opposite, in fact! Even though I want to live at peace with all people, they are a constant reminder that sometimes it just feels impossible. Ugh!

That's why I need Your help so much! When I'm facing those impossible situations, You're right there to guide me this way and that, in and around every problem. You'll show me how to navigate in a way that brings peace and safety to all. No explosions necessary! And somehow, You'll help me do it all without hurting anyone in the process, myself included.

Thank You for being a peace-leading Savior. I'll follow You so that I can live at peace with others, even the toughest cases, Jesus! Amen.

Strength in Quietness
and Trust

*The holy L*ORD *God of Israel had told all of you, "I will*
keep you safe if you turn back to me and calm down.
I will make you strong if you quietly trust me."

ISAIAH 30:15 CEV

Sometimes I get so worked up that I want to shout my complaints to the world, Jesus! It makes me feel better to air my dirty laundry, to let everyone know just how upset I am and why. I would love to pour out all the grimy details, exposing the dirt for what it really is. This is especially true when someone has hurt me or wounded someone I love. Watch out! Grumpy Bear's coming out for a snack!

Then I am reminded of this verse. True peace is found in quietness and trust. That's where I find my strength to overcome those problems that threaten to take me down. Only in quiet time with You will the answers come. Grumpy Bear needs to climb back in her cave and calm down. She needs to trust her Creator to manage things on her behalf.

So I'll bite my tongue. I won't make a big deal out of it. I'll quietly draw near to You and allow You to do that healing work that's important, so that I can come out stronger on the other side. Amen.

The Greatest GPS

Whether you turn to the right or to the left, you will hear a voice saying, "This is the road! Now follow it."

ISAIAH 30:21 CEV

"Do I turn here? No, wait. . .maybe it's the next street. Or the one after that. I can't seem to remember how to get there! Oops!"

How many times have my parents gotten lost while driving? Way too many to count! In those moments, when Mom starts to panic, she's not sure what to do. She ends up pulling the car off the road and checking the GPS app on her phone. Then, once she figures it out, Mom gets back on the road, feeling more confident.

I'm so glad my walk with You isn't like that. I don't have to panic when the road ahead isn't clearly mapped out. I can trust You, even when I can't see what's coming around the next bend. I can have peace in every situation, including those where the ending isn't clear. You're my Guide, Jesus. When I give You every area of my life, You really do straighten my paths. Thank You for being the best GPS ever, Lord! Amen.

A Luscious, Healing Aroma

We should keep on encouraging each other to be
thoughtful and to do helpful things. Some people have
gotten out of the habit of meeting for worship, but
we must not do that. We should keep on encouraging
each other, especially since you know that the
day of the Lord's coming is getting closer.

HEBREWS 10:24–25 CEV

I love the smell of popcorn popping when I walk into the movie theater. There's something pretty heavenly about that yummy aroma. It tickles my senses and makes me giddy! I can't help myself. . .I have to have it! I can almost taste the first bite already.

I want to put off an aroma that is just as pleasing to those around me, Jesus! Instead of the stench of whining and complaining, I want to offer up the fragrance of a peaceful heart, one that brings comfort to those who are struggling and joy to those who are hurting. Before they even see me coming, may the people in my world be encouraged and hopeful. "Hey, it's her! She's going to make everything better!"

I want to reflect You in everything I say and do, a yummy aroma of Your love. Amen.

I Will See Your Loving-Kindness

*I would have been without hope if I had not
believed that I would see the loving-kindness
of the Lord in the land of the living.*

PSALM 27:13 NLV

Sometimes I wonder: *Will I have to wait until I'm in heaven
to see anything good happen?* I feel myself getting pretty
depressed by all the evil around me—in politics, in the way
my friends act, in the not-so-great actions of those who are
trying to hurt me.

Then I'm reminded of this verse, and I realize that I won't
have to wait until I'm in heaven to experience Your goodness.
It surrounds me all day, every day, Jesus!

I see it in the smile of my grandma and notice it in the twinkle in her eye. I witness it in the kindness of a stranger who
stops to help my mom change a tire. I notice when someone
does something extra nice for me just because. I see it every
day if I just pay attention!

Your loving-kindness amazes me. I don't ever want to forget
that You're already at work, sharing it through those around
me. Thank You, Lord! Amen.

You've Got Me Covered

*He will cover you with His wings. And under
His wings you will be safe. He is faithful like
a safe-covering and a strong wall.*

PSALM 91:4 NLV

Our pantry is stocked, Lord! It's filled with every good thing so that we're prepared for the days ahead. We'll never go hungry, that's for sure! There are canned foods, spices, and breakfast cereals. . . . Our refrigerator is loaded with good things too.

It feels good to have everything we need. It feels even better, Lord, to know that You're on the job inside me too! You've filled my heart with all the good things I could ever need: gentleness, peace, goodness, faithfulness, self-control . . . My heart pantry is full, indeed. You've provided all I need. I'll never have to make a quick dash to the store to pick up peace or joy or gentleness. They're all right here, ready for the taking.

I'm so grateful for this amazing provision, Jesus! Thanks for covering me with all I could need—and more. Amen.

Joy I Can't Express

You have never seen Him but you love Him. You cannot see Him now but you are putting your trust in Him. And you have joy so great that words cannot tell about it. You will get what your faith is looking for, which is to be saved from the punishment of sin.

1 PETER 1:8–9 NLV

I love how faith works, Jesus! Even though I can't see, I choose to believe. Even though I don't hear Your actual voice, I feel You speaking to my heart day in and day out, through every situation, good or bad. Because I feel You close by, I'm convinced of Your presence and Your great love.

This kind of faith—trusting what I can't see—brings joy to my heart. I'm living an adventure with You! This faith brings calmness. It brings peace. Why? Because I'm absolutely sure You are near, even when I'm completely alone in a room.

Sounds crazy to others, I guess! No matter what they think, I will continue to believe what I can't see or hear, because I've witnessed Your goodness in my life. And because of what I've witnessed, I truly have supernatural joy!

Keep speaking, Lord! I'm listening. Amen.

I'm Your Child

But to all who did receive him, who believed in his name, he gave the right to become children of God.

JOHN 1:12 ESV

Sometimes I feel like a real whiz in the kitchen, Lord, cooking up all kinds of tasty things for those I love. Cookies. Cupcakes. Special treats. Lots of yummy goodness. My family and friends love it when I go into cooking mode, for sure. They know lots of treats are headed their way!

How fun, to know that You are cooking up even greater things to share with us, Your kids! You have peace, love, joy, goodness, self-control, and so many other wonderful presents in store for us if we will only slow down long enough to take a bite. I get excited, thinking about all the wonderful surprises You have in store!

Today I choose to eat at Your table, to feast with You. You will delight me with sweet treasures. I can hardly wait to see what You've wrapped in ribbons and bows just for me! Amen.

Because I Know You

Everyone who honors your name can trust you,
because you are faithful to all who depend on you.

PSALM 9:10 CEV

I've looked for it under every bush, Lord! I've searched the corners of the rooms, peering through the icky, sticky cobwebs. I've looked under the sofa and in the closets, and I've even searched the attics of my heart. But I never seem to find peace until I come into Your presence.

Because I know You, I can have access to all that You are, all that You will ever be. So I don't have to search for peace as long as I draw near to You. I don't need to pull out a treasure map to find joy. Or faith. Or hope. All I have to do is crawl into Your arms for some one-on-one time with my heavenly Father, and You begin to download exactly what I need.

Because I know You, I have access to all the treasures I could need and much, much more. You thought of everything, Lord! How grateful I am to know You! Amen.

You Finish What You Start

*It is because you have told others the Good
News from the first day you heard it until
now. I am sure that God Who began the good
work in you will keep on working in you
until the day Jesus Christ comes again.*

PHILIPPIANS 1:5–6 NLV

I'm not an unfinished book, Lord! You see all the way through
to the end of my story. Someday, You will finish all the cool
things You started in me when I was a little kid. I can't see
into the future to know how the story will end, but You can!

I wish I had eyes like You. (What are You planning for me,
Lord? Can I have a little peek?)

When things get rough—and they do—I will remember
that the story doesn't end here. There are chapters, already
written, with characters I haven't even met. Adventures
await me as the pages are flipped one to the next. So I won't
give up on the hard days, although I'm tempted to curl up in
a ball and wish the world away.

I'll take Your hand and let You lead me into tomorrow,
secure in the fact that good things are ahead in this precious
story of mine. Amen.

A Tree, Deeply Planted

"Good will come to the man who trusts in the Lord, and whose hope is in the Lord. He will be like a tree planted by the water, that sends out its roots by the river. It will not be afraid when the heat comes but its leaves will be green. It will not be troubled in a dry year, or stop giving fruit."

JEREMIAH 17:7–8 NLV

I just want to thank You today for awesome mentors, Jesus! You have placed a lot of great people in my life! So many times, I've needed the advice or the wisdom of someone who really cares, of someone who knows You. You always send the perfect person just when I need them—one whose faith roots go down deep. A fruit bearer.

It makes me feel good to find a friend who walks closely with You, because I know the advice I receive from her will be well thought out and prayed over. She wants Your best for me, just as You do.

Godly counsel brings peace, especially in these crazy times we are living in. Thank You for these precious, godly mentors. And thank You for using me to mentor others too. Amen.

Oh, So Right!

*The Laws of the Lord are right, giving
joy to the heart. The Word of the Lord
is pure, giving light to the eyes.*

PSALM 19:8 NLV

Following the rules isn't always fun, Jesus! There have been times I've rebelled against them, as You already know. I felt restricted. Trapped! There was no joy during those times, for sure!

Thank goodness You never give me that trapped feeling! Your precepts are life-giving and heart-altering. They're always right—in every situation. They bring joy to my heart and light to my eyes. I wouldn't know how to move forward without them, in fact.

I've never heard of rules that guide me before, Lord, but that's what Yours do! They're a lovely map, all laid out for me. They illuminate my path and give light to my eyes. I would be lost without them.

I won't rebel against Your laws! They are w-a-y too important to wander away from. They are meant for my good, not evil. So, with everything inside of me, I will embrace them as the gift they are and walk in them as best I can. Amen.

Your Steadfast Love

"But I will not remove from him my steadfast love or be false to my faithfulness."

PSALM 89:33 ESV

There's nothing I can do to lose Your love, Jesus. Knowing that brings me such peace! If I go to the heavens, You are there. If I tumble to the deepest, darkest places, You're there too. (This I know from experience, sadly!) Your love provides a soft landing spot for me, even when I color outside the lines or drift into the wrong lane. Yep, I've done that a time or two, I know!

Why do You love me so much? I can't figure that part out. I feel so unlovable at times, but You don't seem to see me that way at all. In fact, You love me so much that You gave Your Son for me. Wow!

How could I ever walk away from such a love, Jesus? I won't! Not now, not ever. If I'm ever tempted, please remind me how deep, how wide, how high, and how vast is that abounding love. It came from heaven to earth just for me! Amen.

Springtime Is Coming!

Each one of you is part of the body of Christ,
and you were chosen to live together in
peace. So let the peace that comes from Christ
control your thoughts. And be grateful.

COLOSSIANS 3:15 CEV

I took a walk this morning, Jesus. I love Your creation! It's so cool to watch blades of grass shoot up from the ground almost like magic. And watching flowers open up and face the sun? So cool!

You've done the same thing in my heart. You've taken dry, cracked places and miraculously watered the soil and planted seeds of hope, joy, and peace. They are sprouting up, even now, bringing hope for a brighter future. I see sprigs of green peeking through!

I didn't think it was possible after the awful stuff I've been through. I thought the soil of my heart would remain cracked and dry forever. Felt that way in the moment. But here I am, Jesus, in a new springtime. And there You are, making sure there's new growth for a great harvest. There are brighter days ahead. I am filled with hope as the earth gives way to newness! Amen.

A Way of Escape

You are tempted in the same way that everyone else is tempted. But God can be trusted not to let you be tempted too much, and he will show you how to escape from your temptations.

1 CORINTHIANS 10:13 CEV

The trashman just showed up. He's loading the stuff we put on the curb, the junk that holds no value anymore. He's hauling it away to the dump, where it will be buried under mounds of dirt, never to be seen again. Get rid of it, I say!

I watch him, and I am reminded of the many times You have carried away the trash bags in my life, Jesus. All those things I once thought I needed? They led only to death and destruction in the end. They robbed me of my peace. They blinded me to the truth.

But then You showed up and gave me clear vision! How wonderful, to let those icky things go. How awesome, to know that You have hauled them off to Your great landfill, to know that You've tossed my sins as far as the east is from the west. I'll never see them again, Lord, and that's just fine with me! Amen.

Peace in Unity

How good and pleasant it is when
God's people live together in unity!

PSALM 133:1 NIV

Sometimes, Jesus, I have something tough to share with someone I care about, and I don't want to do it. So I dance around the subject and try to find an easier way to say what needs to be said. Or I avoid talking about it altogether. It's like an elephant in the room that no one ever mentions.

It would be easier to let someone else step in and do the hard work for me, but You want to grow me into someone who can handle tough conversations. You're teaching me not to be afraid. And You give me the help I need.

I feel Your great peace as I start this tough conversation. Your strength. Your courage. Your hope. I sense them all. Most of all, I'm leaning in close to hear the words You're speaking to my heart so that I can share them with my friend, words filled with love that only You can bring.

Here goes, Lord! Let's do this! Amen.

Shower the Garden of My Heart

The LORD is good to everyone.
He showers compassion on all his creation.

PSALM 145:9 NLT

Jesus, sometimes I feel like my heart is a garden and You are the Master Gardener. You get rid of the weeds that grow—the ones that threaten to choke out any signs of life. And You plant my roots in You down deep so that I can blossom and grow, despite any changes in the conditions around me. (And boy, do they ever change from day to day!)

I'm sorry for the times I've just skimmed the surface of our relationship. When I allow that to happen, I grow weak in faith. I lose my peace and wonder why. But I know why! It's because I've secluded myself far from You. I don't allow You to till the soil of my heart. I don't let my roots run deep, as I should.

But those days are behind me now! Today I invite You back in to tend to this dry, cracked soil. Nurture, saturate, and tend to me as only You can, Lord. Soften the soil so that the roots can go way, way down to the deepest places with You, I pray. Amen.

When I'm Tired and Weighed Down, I Come

If you are tired from carrying heavy burdens,
come to me and I will give you rest.

MATTHEW 11:28 CEV

I've carried some pretty heavy burdens, Lord. They weigh me down. But I don't always shake them off easily. Sometimes I carry that weight like a badge of honor. I show it off to others instead of getting rid of it once and for all.

Maybe it helps me get attention or causes people to feel sorry for me. I don't know. I just know that releasing those burdens isn't as easy as I thought it would be.

You tell me that I need to come to You, Lord. When I take the time to do that, You fix the problems I'm facing in Your way and Your time. "Coming" requires action on my part, and sometimes I simply get stuck.

Help me get unstuck, I pray. I want to do as You ask, Father, so that I can have true and lasting peace. I will give You those things I've held so tightly to, once and for all! Amen.

My Times Are in Your Hands

But as for me, I trust in You, O Lord. I say,
"You are my God." My times are in Your hands.
Free me from the hands of those who hate
me, and from those who try to hurt me.

PSALM 31:14–15 NLV

You're not ruled by the clock, are You, Jesus? You have a completely different way of looking at time than I do. It's so cool that You saw my life before I was even conceived. Long before then, You knew me and You loved me. Wow!

It's amazing to think that You know where I'm headed next, who I will meet, where I will go, and how my life will unfold until I'm with You in heaven. There are times when I wish I could peek behind the curtain and see all of that too. Other times, I'm glad I don't see!

Still, knowing that You know every detail gives me peace. It really builds my trust in You to know that You're the Maker of my days from beginning to end. So the things I'm worried about right now? They're just a blip in the grand scheme of things. Heaven is waiting for me, where I'll spend eternity with You.

Until then, it brings me peace to know my days are in Your hands, Lord! I'm super grateful for Your timeless love. Amen.

Consistent. . .Like You

*Jesus Christ is the same yesterday
and today and forever.*

HEBREWS 13:8 ESV

I never saw that attack coming, Jesus! When it hit, my response was a little ungodly, to say the least. Lack of trust, fear, panic. . .all those things and more swept over me. I blew it! So much for being a girl of great faith! My peace went right out the window, and I acted like a hopeless person. I'm ashamed of my knee-jerk reaction. What happened to being consistent? Ugh!

Thank You for not letting me stay there. You took me back to Your Word, where I was reminded that You never change. You're never thrown off by problems, Jesus. You remain steady as a rock, day in and day out. Yesterday. Today. Forever. You're always and forever the same. Steady. Consistent. Permanent. Unbending. That's the kind of God You are, and it's the kind of woman I long to become.

Today, I put my trust in You and recommit myself to consistency in my faith walk. Help me, I pray! Amen.

I Will Make Every Effort

And so God's people have a complete rest waiting
for them. The man who goes into God's rest, rests
from his own work the same as God rested from
His work. Let us do our best to go into that rest
or we will be like the people who did not go in.

HEBREWS 4:9–11 NLV

It's so ironic that rest sometimes feels like work, Jesus. It would be easier if I could just relax and enjoy a day off with You. But I'm always on the go, go, go! Slowing down? Yeah, not so much! It goes against my nature. I'm like a bee, buzzing from here to there. (There's so much to do!)

You must have known I would be like this. That's why You cover the topic of rest in the Bible. You knew it wouldn't come naturally to some of us. Okay, me.

I don't always need to go, go, go, Lord. Teach me how to experience Your rest, I pray. I want to be refreshed and invigorated for the journey ahead, and that can only happen as I lay down the busyness and draw near to You. Amen.

Every Good Gift

Whatever is good and perfect is a gift coming down to us from God our Father, who created all the lights in the heavens. He never changes or casts a shifting shadow.

JAMES 1:17 NLT

I love all Your amazing creations, Jesus. Ladybugs. Caterpillars. Seahorses. Autumn leaves. I marvel at how detailed they are! These things are just a few of the gifts You've given us to enjoy.

I also love sunrises, sunsets, puffy clouds, ocean waves, and so much more. I stand in awe as I gaze at each one, and I'm reminded of Your great creative powers. No one makes things like You do, Lord. Wow!

It brings great peace to my heart to realize that the almighty Author of all things—the most magnificent Creator—thought He needed one of *me* too. You couldn't do without me, Lord! That makes me smile. You loved me so much that You gave me all of creation to enjoy, a gift from Your heart to mine.

We will enjoy it together, Jesus—mountain peaks, rushing rivers, even the valleys. Everything You've created will be appreciated and loved! Amen.

Father, I Come

*It is better to trust in the Lord
than to trust in man.*

PSALM 118:8 NLV

Jesus, You want me to hang out with You all day long—every minute, every hour, every day! (Hey, no one else wants to spend that much time with me, so thank You!) You want me to stick close. It's not always easy. Sometimes I have to shift my attention from the many things that are calling my name—school, family, friends, my messy room. . .Whew! The distractions are everywhere!

I'll admit it. . .sometimes it's hard for me to just be. I would rather be going, going, going, doing, doing, doing. I forget that the distractions can wait and that spending time with You is the most important part of each day.

During our hanging-out times, You fill my heart with such peace, such joy! Why would I put that off? I can't find those things when I'm rushing around in a frenzy. I don't sense them when my eyes are focused on stuff going on around me. But when I take the time to hang out with You, peace like a river washes over me. Let's hang out more, Jesus! Amen.

Sweeter Than Honey

The fear of the Lord is pure, lasting forever. The Lord is always true and right in how He judges. The Word of the Lord is worth more than gold, even more than much fine gold. They are sweeter than honey, even honey straight from the comb.

PSALM 19:9–10 NLV

I can see it now, Jesus. . .honey dripping from the honeycomb. Mmm! That sweet, nourishing goodness reminds me of You—of Your laws, Your Word, Your kindness. I'm guided by Your goodness. And once I get started with something sweet, watch out! I just want more and more.

That's what I'm asking from You today, Lord—more of You. More of Your Word, Your thoughts, Your hope, Your peace.

When I'm tempted to taste the things of this world (and boy, is there a lot out there!), please remind me that the only lasting peace I will ever find is in what You have to offer. The world is full of counterfeits, nothing more. So I will stick with You, Jesus! Your Word truly is more precious than gold and sweeter than honey. Amen.

Wherever I Go

*"Have I not commanded you? Be strong and courageous.
Do not be frightened, and do not be dismayed, for
the LORD your God is with you wherever you go."*

JOSHUA 1:9 ESV

Who turned the lights out, Jesus? Sometimes it seems like I'm staggering around in the dark, unable to find my way. My sense of direction is gone. My hope fades. My peace is shaken!

Then, suddenly, You come on the scene. Everything is lit up. I take confident steps forward, knowing that You are lighting my path and guiding me into the vast unknown. Right away, my courage returns. I'm strong. I'm brave. I'm not frightened by the shadows or by things that go bump in the night. Hope is restored and discouragement fades, and all because I know You're guiding me!

It brings me such peace, to walk in Your radiant light with Your hand in mine. How I praise You for loving and guiding me wherever I go. Amen.

Calm Down!

*A hot-tempered person stirs up conflict,
but the one who is patient calms a quarrel.*

PROVERBS 15:18 NIV

The teakettle on the stove is hissing, threatening to boil over. I know exactly how it feels. I've been there many times lately. I've let my temper get the best of me. It has bubbled to the surface, threatening to spew on anyone who walks by. I've been a hazard not just to others but even to myself.

There are people in my life, Lord—You know the ones. They bring me to a boil quicker than anyone else. Ugh. I don't know why they grate on me like they do. I confess that I struggle most with them. But I don't want to. I want peaceful, loving relationships, even with the tough cases!

Calm my heart, I pray. Bring peace. Rid me of this anger, this temper, once and for all. I give this bubbling heart to You, Lord, and ask You to do what only You can: calm things down! Lower the temperature. Bring that boil to a gentle simmer so that I can love others as You love them. Boy, do I need Your help with this one! Amen.

Complete Confidence!

I am glad I can have complete confidence in you.

2 CORINTHIANS 7:16 NIV

I'll admit it, Lord: I've messed up a lot of things, w-a-y too many to count. (I'm so glad You don't keep track!)

Some days I look at the puzzle of my life and feel like half the pieces are missing. I've made a huge mess of things. And it's my own doing. I've carelessly tossed the puzzle box in the air, allowing the pieces to fall wherever. I didn't listen to You. I didn't follow Your instructions. No wonder I was such a hot mess!

But You? You're the great Puzzle Maker. You know exactly where the missing pieces are. You found a few in the ditch. You noticed a couple more when I had a crush on that boy at school. And You found even more in that horrible situation I faced with my grades.

Then You supplied the biggest piece of all, the One I'd been missing all along. You, Jesus! You're the missing piece. It all makes sense now. The story wasn't complete until You came into it.

So put me back together, I pray. I can't wait to see this amazing picture You're creating! Amen.

Feet in Quicksand

*We can come to God without fear because
we have put our trust in Christ.*

EPHESIANS 3:12 NLV

I feel stuck. Like feet-in-quicksand stuck, Jesus! I can't figure out if I should turn to the right or the left. Should I move? Should I stay put? What should I do? Oh, help! If I stand here much longer, I'll go under. Then what?

I know, I know. . .I've been through seasons like this before. But right now, I feel like I'm frozen in place, unable to make a decision. And this quicksand is getting deeper by the minute! I need Your perspective on this situation so that I'll know what to do. I'm afraid of making a mistake, one that can't be unmade.

Help me? Please, Lord. I don't want to do something now that will need to be corrected later. So, give me the wisdom—right now, in this moment—to do the right thing. Then I'll have true and lasting peace. I won't make a move until I hear from You, Lord. Amen.

Who's Your Boss?

If your sinful old self is the boss over your mind,
it leads to death. But if the Holy Spirit is the boss
over your mind, it leads to life and peace.

ROMANS 8:6 NLV

How many times have I longed for things I shouldn't have, Jesus? A million? Ten million? That huge piece of chocolate cake, when I shouldn't be eating so many sugary things? That gorgeous new phone, the one I can't really afford? That relationship that's going to end up pulling me away from You?

These cravings to have whatever I want in the moment? They're not bringing me much peace, Lord. The more I want, want, want, the less satisfied I am in You. It's a vicious cycle, one that needs to be broken before I find myself completely lost.

Help me find peace with what I already have, Lord. You've blessed me so much already. May I find true joy and satisfaction in the good gifts You've already poured out. I don't want to waste my days searching for that "next big thing" when I already have the best of all. You've given me all I could ever want and more. I'm so grateful. Amen.

A Different Thought Process

"For my thoughts are not your thoughts,
neither are your ways my ways," declares the LORD.

ISAIAH 55:8 NIV

I just don't get some people, Jesus! The way they process things, the way they act. . .it confuses me! I have a completely different way of thinking, of doing things.

I guess that's what makes us unique. I have one studying style; she has another. I have one way of speaking to my friends; she has another. I keep my bedroom looking one way; she keeps hers looking another.

As different as we are, we're even more different than You! Your thoughts are so far beyond mine that I can't even begin to figure out how You do things. How did You fling the stars into space? How did You settle on the length of a giraffe's neck? How did You decide that roses needed thorns?

There are so many things about You that make me curious, Lord. But I have all of eternity to observe and to try to become more like You. Thanks for being uniquely You! Amen.

Be Still and Know

"Be still, and know that I am God. I will be exalted among the nations, I will be exalted in the earth!"

PSALM 46:10 ESV

Jesus, You say that I can know You. . .if I will only be still.

That's my problem right there! Slowing down long enough to actually be still is an issue for me, if I'm being honest. I like to run on warp speed much of the time. Slowing down doesn't come naturally. And when I do stop, I usually crash. I'm out like a light a few minutes later.

But if it's true that I will know You as God if I will just slow down, then slow down I will. Because I want to know You—fully, totally, completely. I want to see You exalted among the nations. I want to see Your kingdom come and Your will be done.

Only in fully coming to know You will I have lasting peace in my heart. I need that, Lord, and not just to get through the busy seasons! And I know others need it too, so I will remain serious about my pledge to slow down so that I can lead by example.

I praise You, Lord! Be exalted in my (busy!) heart. Amen.

I Wish I May

*Deep in my heart I long for your temple,
and with all that I am I sing joyful songs to you.*

PSALM 84:2 CEV

"I wish I may, I wish I might, have the wish I wish tonight."
How many times did I say that little poem when I was a kid?
Back then, I really thought that all my dreams and wishes
would come true. I thought You were some sort of genie in
a bottle, Jesus. I was sure You were there to fulfill my wants
and wishes, to meet—not every need—but every want.

Sometimes I still look at You that way, if I'm being totally
honest. I want what I want. . .and I want it on my time-
table. "I wish I may, I wish I might. . .Lord, please grant my
wish tonight!"

You're so gracious, Jesus! You don't get mad at me when
I come to You with my wish list. Even when I'm worked up
and irritated because things didn't come together like I'd
hoped, You show me grace and mercy. Instead of scolding,
You graciously receive me and give me, not what I want but
what I need.

Turn my heart, Jesus! I want to desire You alone, not the
things You can give me. Amen.

Equipped

*All Scripture is breathed out by God and profitable
for teaching, for reproof, for correction, and for
training in righteousness, that the man of God may
be complete, equipped for every good work.*

2 TIMOTHY 3:16–17 ESV

You wouldn't ask me to do something unless You prepared me
for it, Jesus. You must think I'm ready, or I wouldn't be here!
Sure, my knees are knocking and my voice is quivering, but
knowing You've placed me here gives me courage.

I'm guessing You've been getting me ready for this very
moment for a while now. You've prepped my heart and given
me everything I need, not only to get through this situation
but to succeed in the process. Through Your Word and my life
experiences, You've been teaching, training, and tutoring!
So I will stand confident and filled with peace as I draw in a
deep breath and step forward. I won't give in to fear. I'll just
look to You to do what I can't. Thanks for equipping me with
Your Word, and thank You for going before me as I bravely
step forward. Amen.

Not as the World Gives

"Peace I leave with you; my peace I give to you.
Not as the world gives do I give to you. Let not your
hearts be troubled, neither let them be afraid."

JOHN 14:27 ESV

Yap, yap, yap! The neighbor's dog won't stop barking. The yapping is getting on my nerves and making me lose my peace. Should I say something? Do something?

Then just like that, I'm reminded of all the many times I have yap-yap-yapped to my friends and family members: "My life is awful. Everything is terrible. Etc. Etc. Etc." On and on and on I go, complaining about this circumstance or that circumstance. I invite them to my pity party, and I'm the guest of honor.

Of course, every time I do this, I'm messing up my own peace of mind as well as the peace of those I'm complaining to! They probably don't need all my drama, especially when I still haven't taken the advice they offered the last time.

Calm my heart, Jesus! Stop the yapping. Remind me that I can turn to You. You're able to handle me even when I'm a hot mess. Let's spare my friends the drama. I don't want to be that annoying friend everyone runs from. But I need Your help with this one. (Actually, I need Your help with all of it!) Amen.

You Calm the Storms

*But Jesus replied, "Why are you so afraid?
You surely don't have much faith." Then he
got up and ordered the wind and the waves
to calm down. And everything was calm.*

MATTHEW 8:26 CEV

At times it feels like there's a volcano in my heart, Jesus. I can feel it rumbling, rumbling, rumbling, threatening to erupt. At any moment now, it's going to blow, and the fallout will be shocking. Devastating. I'm going to take out whole villages with the eruption. Or at least tear down those I love. That's my fear, anyway. I can see the potential for disaster as my insides tremble like hot lava.

What can calm the volcano? What can settle the rumble, put out the fire? Only You, Lord. When I'm stirred up like this, You can step in and rebuke the winds and the waves. You can calm the fury raging inside of me. You can, with one word, push the lava back down into the volcano. In fact, You can cool things down to the point where that volcano never blows again.

I need Your help, Jesus! Calm the storms in me, I pray. Bring peace to this heart of mine. Amen.

Overcomer!

*For everyone who has been born of God
overcomes the world. And this is the victory
that has overcome the world—our faith.*

1 JOHN 5:4 ESV

There have been moments when I've been in so much pain, physically and emotionally, that I couldn't bear it any longer. I got overwhelmed, Jesus. I wanted to give up.

When that kind of pain hits, the enemy tries to slip through the cracks of my soul to tell me that the pain will never end. He whispers in my ear, "God doesn't care. If He cared, you wouldn't be going through this."

But I won't listen to his voice today! No matter how much pain I face, I will look to You, the One who can bring peace and hope into my life. There is a path out of this pain. I will trust You as we walk it, hand in hand. You are teaching me how to overcome. Your Word says that everyone who has been born of God overcomes the world.

I've been born of God! That means I'm going to get through this. There will be victory on the other side, Lord. I'm believing for that even now. Amen.

I Want to Please You

*Let my words and my thoughts be pleasing to you, LORD,
because you are my mighty rock and my protector.*

PSALM 19:14 CEV

I can't make up my mind about the temperature, Lord! One minute I'm hot and pulling off my sweater. The next minute I'm freezing and ready to turn on the heater.

I guess the same thing could be said about my temperament. Some days I'm cool, calm, and collected. Other days I'm like a hot tamale! I seem to switch back and forth, never knowing where the day will take me. You want the words of my mouth and the meditation of my heart to be pleasing in Your sight. That's not always the case on the "hot" days.

You're very patient, to love me through the back-and-forth struggles. You somehow bring peace whether I'm running hot or cold. And You offer forgiveness for the (many!) times I'm a hot mess. I want to please You. I really do! So protect my heart and help me remain steady, I pray. Thank You, Jesus! Amen.

Hovering over the Waters

*Now the earth was formless and empty, darkness
was over the surface of the deep, and the Spirit
of God was hovering over the waters.*

GENESIS 1:2 NIV

Some days I feel like I'm in the desert, parched and dry. I'm like the earth before creation, formless and empty. Other days Your peace washes over me like a waterfall, freely pouring. I'm like the oceans just after creation, full to overflowing! Oh, how I love those days!

I can almost imagine what it was like at creation when Your Spirit hovered over the waters as they were formed. That's how I feel on those days when I'm standing in the flow of Your goodness and Your holy peace.

Today I open myself up to Your river. Take the cracked, parched places of my heart. Take every unsettled feeling, every hurt, every misunderstanding. Apply Your peace like an ointment over my wounded soul. Hover overhead as You form something new in my heart.

I open myself up to that amazing waterfall, Lord. I'm ready! Amen.

Found Faithful

"Who is the faithful and wise servant whom
his owner has made boss over the other servants?
He is to have food ready for them at the right time.
That servant is happy who is doing what his owner
wants him to do when he comes back. For sure, I tell
you, he will make him boss over all that he has."

MATTHEW 24:45–47 NLV

Life seems to run in seasons. I have seasons of lack and seasons of plenty. Seasons when life moves along at a s-l-o-w pace and seasons when everything seems to be whizzing by me. Whew!

There are seasons when I trust You completely, Jesus, and other seasons when I hide myself away, cowering in fear. I forget that You're trustworthy, and I cringe like a helpless baby.

Help me to tell one season from the other so that I can live a peaceful life no matter what's swirling around me. I will not be controlled by the shifting winds—the hot, the cold, the lukewarm—because I know who controls the seasons. You're in control of it all, just like You're in control of my heart. I want to be found faithful in trusting You, Lord! Amen.

Always of Good Courage

We are sure of this. We know that while we are at home in this body we are not with the Lord. Our life is lived by faith. We do not live by what we see in front of us.

2 CORINTHIANS 5:6-7 NLV

I need faith to overcome this crazy world I'm living in, Jesus! I need courage to see past the chaos swirling around me—at school and on social media. It's a good thing I don't put my hope in people. They are filled with opinions, and most don't match up with Your Word. I'm also glad I don't have to put my faith in politics. What a mess that would be! Division, chaos, fighting about every little difference of opinion? No thanks!

I don't even put my trust in the church, though I love my church. I've seen the good, the bad, and the ugly, even in my own church friends. No, Lord, there's really only one place I can put my trust. . .in You. During crazy times, I will stay courageous as I place my trust right where it belongs—in the only One who has never let me down! Thanks for that, Jesus! Amen.

The Day Was Made for Me

Then he said to them, "The Sabbath was made
for man, not man for the Sabbath."

MARK 2:27 NIV

Lately I've been dragging, Jesus. I'm feeling sluggish, like someone pulled the plug and drained all my "zap!" and "zow!"

I look at the people around me and wonder where they get all the energy they have. They must be taking some amazing vitamins! Then I'm reminded that my zapped energy is probably tied to a life that's out of balance. Good food, the right amount of sleep, balance of schoolwork and play—these areas of my life could use some serious work!

I really want Your peace, but I know it will only come when my strength is from You. So today I'm asking You for supernatural power so that I can have good health—physically, mentally, and emotionally. Help me rest so that I can be restored and refreshed. You created the Sabbath for me, Lord. I want to rest from my labors and enjoy the day. Amen.

I Will Love Forever!

*I have written these things to you who believe
in the name of the Son of God. Now you can
know you have life that lasts forever.*

1 JOHN 5:13 NLV

Sometimes I think about the word *forever*, Jesus. It seems unimaginable that my life could go on and on and on, past time itself. But with You, there are no ticking clocks, no second hands marching, marching, marching along. You're a "forever" God, One who loved me even before I came into this world. (Wow!)

Eternity is too much for my mind to figure out, but You have written it on my heart. I'm reminded of this: every time I go through something hard, it won't last forever. Only one thing lasts forever, and that's eternity with You. Because I've believed in Your name, because I've asked You to be mine forever, we'll have a relationship that transcends time.

I'll never understand it, Lord, but maybe I wasn't meant to. Instead, I'll just enjoy my forever time with You. Amen.

Hidden Away in My Heart

I will do right and praise you by
learning to respect your perfect laws.

PSALM 119:7 CEV

There are times when I feel like my heart is filled with secret chambers, Lord. There are rooms hidden away that only You can see. I've done an amazing job of hiding them from others, as You know!

In those rooms, I have stored pains, hurts, worries, painful memories, and a few good things too. They're all carefully tucked away, safely kept for me and me alone. If anyone else found them, I don't know what I would do.

Of course, there are days when I wish I could hire a house cleaner to come and tidy up those rooms, to clear them of the junk. I would definitely feel better if they were taken care of once and for all.

Will You do that for me today, please? I give You permission to enter the secret chambers and heal me as only You can so that I might find true and lasting peace even in the deepest places. Help me, I pray. Amen.

You Know Me Well

You know when I am resting or when I am working,
and from heaven you discover my thoughts.

PSALM 139:2 CEV

Where is my heart most comfortable? Good question, Jesus! I searched for a home with my friends. Nothing lasted long. I searched for a home in my talents and abilities. There was some satisfaction but nothing permanent. I searched for it in guilty pleasures that lasted for a little while. But they faded quickly.

I even looked for a place for my heart to live in the past—in the deep, dark painful moments I've experienced. Thank goodness, pain wasn't meant to be my permanent dwelling place!

No, I could not find a home until I came face-to-face with You, Lord! There, my heart finally found its resting place. I am Yours forever. I am home forever. And in this precious home I am known. In fact, You know everything about me—when I sit, when I rise, even what I'm thinking. How amazing to be home at last with the One who loves me most. Amen.

Though the Earth Give Way

And so, we won't be afraid! Let the earth tremble
and the mountains tumble into the deepest sea.

PSALM 46:2 CEV

Life is filled with troubles. I'll be honest, Jesus: Sometimes it feels completely unfair that the people I love have to deal with so many tragedies, problems, and pains. My heart goes out to them. I do my best to comfort them, but what can I say except to point them to You, which should always be my first response?

Your Word says, "And so, we won't be afraid! Let the earth tremble and the mountains tumble into the deepest sea." Trembling earth, tumbling mountains. . .that's a lot of negative action coming against us! But if You promise in Your Word that catastrophes can strike and I can somehow rise above them, I will choose to believe Your Word! It has never failed me, after all.

I pray the earth doesn't give way. I pray these difficult situations will resolve. But even if they don't, Father, I will still choose to love and follow You. And I will continue to believe that You will give me peace, even during the shaking. Thank You for that promise! Amen.

Your Rod and Staff Comfort Me

Even though I walk through the darkest valley,
I will fear no evil, for you are with me;
your rod and your staff, they comfort me.

PSALM 23:4 NIV

I think about the sheep in the field, the little naughty ones that don't want to do as they are told. The shepherd calls them, but they refuse to obey. So he takes the rod and gently leads them where they need to go. What a gentle, loving shepherd he is, more concerned about the animals' safety than anything else.

Sometimes I'm like one of those little sheep, Jesus. I wander to the edge of the field and look off into the distance, wishing for other places to roam. *What would life be like over there?* I wonder. Then You show up, Jesus! You nudge me with Your staff and guide me back to the right path. You're my Good Shepherd! You don't use Your rod and staff to hurt or abuse me but to love me back to where I need to go. With Your gentle touch, You bring peace and remind me that one day with You is better than a thousand elsewhere. Thanks for leading me so gently, Jesus! Amen.

I Won't Add Fuel to the Fire

And above all these put on love, which binds
everything together in perfect harmony.

COLOSSIANS 3:14 ESV

She hurt my feelings, Jesus! She said things that hurt—a lot. She didn't even offer those words with kindness! Instead, she flung them at me with no care at all, deliberately intending to wound me. Those horrible words hit their mark, and now I'm hurting. There's no peace in my heart today because I want to snap back. I want to say all the things that are on my mind. I've been building up quite a speech in my head! Oh, if only I could spew those words at her. Then they would hit their mark too!

But I won't, Jesus. Instead, I choose to bite my tongue and respond as You would respond so that I can live at peace with all people. I'll keep my distance. I've learned a hard lesson with this friend, and I'll know how to handle her in the future. But I won't add fuel to an already blazing fire. Amen.

The Meditation of My Heart

My mouth will speak wisdom. And the
thoughts of my heart will be understanding.

PSALM 49:3 NLV

I pop my vitamins in my mouth, 100 percent convinced they will make me stronger, healthier, and more active. I eat healthy food, knowing it will give me the nutrients I need to get through the day. So why do I forget to run to Your Word, to taste the goodness buried in those pages?

The Bible says that my mouth can speak words of wisdom. (Cool! I'm counting on it!) But Jesus, I know that can only happen if I've actually spent enough time reading my Bible to absorb those words. How can they come out of me if they haven't gone in?

So I turn to Your Word today. I eat it. I drink it. I allow it to wash over me, to go to the deepest places. Only then am I ready to speak life to others. And that's exactly what I want to do! Amen.

Sharing It with Others

A servant must be faithful to his owner.
This is expected of him.

1 CORINTHIANS 4:2 NLV

I want to be faithful to You, Jesus, no matter what! After all, You've given me so much, and I'm super grateful. Now I want to give back! I want to live a faithful life, sharing what I've learned with others along the way.

You've shown me how to walk in peace even through difficult situations. You've given me joy for the journey. You've taught me that I can rise above my circumstances. You've blessed me beyond belief! (Thank You!)

Now show me how I can speak boldly about my faith to others so that they can have joy, peace, and confidence as they face challenges in their lives too. I want to be a light, shining for You. After all You've given me, it's the least I can do! Help me, I pray. Amen.

Abounding in Hope

May the God of hope fill you with all joy and peace in believing, so that by the power of the Holy Spirit you may abound in hope.

ROMANS 15:13 ESV

It's a brand-new day, Jesus! A new morning. A fresh start. A clean slate. How bright and beautiful everything looks! How new everything feels! All the worries of yesterday are behind me now, and today is like a new song that hasn't been sung yet. Instead of coming into this day loaded up with worries about yesterday's mistakes, I'm doing the opposite. I'm loaded with hope because I know things can be different today. They can be better. . .more peaceful.

Right now, I give my anxieties, worries, and desires to You so that I can walk with peace in my heart. No looking back. No stressing about tomorrow. I want the joy that only You can bring and the hope that a stress-free day will offer.

You have filled me with all joy and peace in believing that today really can be different, but it's only by the power of Your Spirit, Jesus! So fill me now, I pray. Amen.

Sweet Sleep

When you lie down, you will not be afraid;
when you lie down, your sleep will be sweet.

PROVERBS 3:24 NIV

I watch a newborn baby in her mother's arms, and I'm reminded that You want to bring peace to my heart in much the same way. We can trust You to hold us close and sing away our troubles, Lord, no matter what we're going through.

Your Word says that when I lie down, I don't have to be afraid of anything. I don't need to worry about that big math test coming up. I don't have to fret over the argument with my BFF. I don't have to worry about my mom's financial problems. Instead, my sleep will be sweet, just like a baby's is when cradled in her mama's arms.

Thank You for the reminder that the whole world goes away when I spend time in the safety and protection of Your loving arms. I want to be like that newborn, blissfully unaware of any chaos swirling around me, so content in Your presence that nothing else matters. Amen.

I Learn from Your Goodness

You are good and You do good.
Teach me Your Law.

PSALM 119:68 NLV

I hear the birds singing their joy song in the tree just outside my bedroom window. High above the craziness of this world, they hang out in their nest, completely safe, free to sing to their hearts' content. I want to be that peaceful, Jesus! I want to be lifted above the turmoil and chaos that I face every single day—at school, with my friends, and sometimes even with my family.

The Bible says that You are good and You do *only* good. (Wow!) I always seem to forget that! I stop singing my joy song because I'm weighed down with life. I forget that You've got everything under control. Help me learn from Your goodness, Lord. Seal it on my heart. I don't ever want to forget that You created me to soar above those circumstances. Make me like those birds—carefree as they soar back to their nests.

Today I choose to spend my hours in flight, set free because of Your great love. Amen.

You Are Greater!

When I am afraid, I will trust in You. I praise the Word of God. I have put my trust in God. I will not be afraid. What can only a man do to me? All day long they change my words to say what I did not say. They are always thinking of ways to hurt me. They go after me as in a fight. They hide themselves. They watch my steps, as they have waited to take my life. Because they are bad, do not let them get away. Bring down the people in Your anger, O God.

PSALM 56:3-7 NLV

My enemies came after me a hundred miles an hour, Jesus! Ugh! But You lifted me in Your arms and protected me from them all. Those tricksters couldn't take me down, not with You on the job. They've got their plans, their schemes, but You've been one step ahead of them every single time. Now I stand in complete peace, trusting the One who lifts me above the battle. The One who goes before me. The One with the master plan. (Thanks, Lord!)

There is no enemy greater than my awesome God. So, when fear sets in, when my knees start to knock or my hands tremble, remind me of all the battles You've already won. My faith will grow as I'm reminded. And then, together, we'll show that enemy a thing or two! Amen.

Lead Me to the Rock

I feel hopeless, and I cry out to you from a faraway land. Lead me to the mighty rock high above me.

PSALM 61:2 CEV

I love this verse, Jesus! On days when I'm feeling totally hopeless, lead me to the Rock. On the days when I'm mad at my friend, frustrated with my teacher, worried about my grades. . .lead me to the Rock. On the days when I wander to the farthest corners of the earth, when my heart says, "I'm done. I'm giving up," lead me to the Rock.

Lead me to You, Jesus! Lead me to the safe place with no shifting sand, no hurricane-force winds to knock me down. But even if the winds do come, I know that You will keep me standing as long as I stand firmly planted on You and You alone. My heart might grow faint, but You can take that faint heart and breathe new life in it again, if I will just come to You.

Lead me to the Rock, Lord.

Lead me to You.

Steady, unmoving You. Amen.

Transformed!

Don't be like the people of this world, but let God change the way you think. Then you will know how to do everything that is good and pleasing to him.

ROMANS 12:2 CEV

I've been thinking about how a butterfly comes out of its cocoon, Jesus. The transformation is remarkable to witness. The butterfly starts so tiny, so enclosed, but ends up spreading its wings and flying away from what once held it bound.

Sometimes I'm a little bit like that butterfly. I let fear hold me in its grip. I give away my peace. I'd rather stay in that tight, painful place because breaking free seems too dangerous. Impossible, even.

I'm learning, though! Nothing is impossible with You. You set the little butterfly free, and You long to set me free too. With the breath of Your Spirit, I'm transformed. The fear is lifted. The graveclothes give way, and I'm free to soar—off into new places, new experiences.

Thank You for growing me, Father. Thank You for the transformation process, no matter how scary. I don't want to stay the same. Like that tiny butterfly, I want to soar free. Amen.

Noisy Joy

Praise him with the sounding of the trumpet,
praise him with the harp and lyre,
praise him with timbrel and dancing,
praise him with the strings and pipe,
praise him with the clash of cymbals,
praise him with resounding cymbals.

PSALM 150:3–5 NIV

Noisy joy. How fun! I love that idea.

Your Word tells us to lift Your name in praise, Jesus. . .to make a joyful noise throughout the earth. I'm not always very loud with my praise, but You're helping me get over my shyness. You're showing me that time spent praising You (loudly or otherwise) is good!

When I take the time to praise You, I'm not *just* blessing You; I'm also reminding myself of who You are. You're the One I place my trust in. You're my hiding place. You're my peace. You're the Giver of all good gifts. And You're the only One who truly sees, knows, and loves me for who I am.

So today I choose to lift Your name. I praise You, Jesus! I celebrate this precious life You've given me, and I give You all my worship. You are my King of kings, my Lord of lords, my everything. You are worthy to be praised today and every day! Amen.

The Bond of Peace

*Work hard to live together as one by the help
of the Holy Spirit. Then there will be peace.*

EPHESIANS 4:3 NLV

They're arguing again, Jesus. Why can't they ever get along? I love these people and wish they cared enough about each other to knock it off. Don't they see what they're doing, how this chaos between the two of them isn't messing up just their peace, but mine too? Do they even care? (It sure doesn't feel like it!)

I want to work hard on relationships so that I can live at peace with others. It's the only way to live in total freedom. But those around me don't seem to feel the same way. I think they get a kick out of fighting!

Please enter the hearts of the troubled ones and bring peace. Your Word promises it's possible! I want them to learn to forgive each other just like You've forgiven them. Show me how to be a good influence on those around me who are fighting. Bring peace to the hearts of those I love. Amen.

The Opinions of Others

Obviously, I'm not trying to win the approval of people, but of God. If pleasing people were my goal, I would not be Christ's servant.

GALATIANS 1:10 NLT

Why do I care so much about what other people think of me, Jesus? It shouldn't bother me as much as it does. But I hyperfocus on their opinions. Do they think I'm nice? Do they like the way I look? Do they think I'm always saying or doing the wrong thing? On and on I go, worrying about their opinions of me and imagining what they must be saying once I'm gone from the room.

If I'm being honest, sometimes I put their opinions above Yours. I don't mean to. Maybe I just want to fit in? I'm not sure. But one thing *is* for sure: this isn't a very peaceful way to live, always wondering if people are judging me. Please take this burden away, God! I repent of worrying about the opinions of others. From now on, the only One I will aim to please is You, Lord. Amen.

Your Goodness
Passes Before Me

And God said, "I will have My goodness pass in front of you. I will make the name of the Lord known in front of you. I will have loving-kindness and loving-pity for anyone I want to."

EXODUS 33:19 NLV

I know that You are good, Jesus. I know that You are my only hope. I've witnessed Your favor, Your amazing rescues, more times than I can count. I've seen You work miracles and part the seas just for me!

Why do I always forget? How can I walk away from Your goodness and doubt that You truly care for me? You've never shown one moment of not caring. All I have ever known from You is goodness, peace, love, and joy. That time when I was sick? You were good. That other time, when my parents couldn't pay the mortgage? You sent a surprise package in the mail, a check that covered the bill!

Oh, the stories I could tell if I would just take the time to remember them all. They give me hope and peace for what I'm facing now. Today, Lord, I choose to never forget. I don't want to ever lose hope in the only One who has never let me down. Amen.

Dwell in Safety

I will lie down and sleep in peace.
O Lord, You alone keep me safe.

PSALM 4:8 NLV

You see me, Jesus! You see my tears in the night. You see my struggles in the daytime. You see the fear when I'm facing something scary. You see the joy when I'm with those I love. You see the troubles that are yet to come, and You see the victories in front of me. I can trust You, Lord, and I can have peace because I know that You have twenty-twenty supernatural vision.

Best of all, You see during those dark, lonely hours when I'm tossing and turning, worrying about this or that. When I'm nervous about every little thing that goes bump in the night. When I'm losing sleep over the troubles of the day.

Yes, You see me in the night (with Your terrific night vision!), and You comfort me. You bring peace. You make me feel safe. Only when I feel safe and secure can I (finally!) roll over and go to sleep. How awesome to be safely cared for by You, Lord. Amen.

I Will Learn from You

"Follow My teachings and learn from Me.
I am gentle and do not have pride.
You will have rest for your souls."

MATTHEW 11:29 NLV

You are mighty in battle, Jesus. You're the most amazing warrior ever!

Me? Not so much! Sometimes the armor looks so heavy that I refuse to put it on. It's cumbersome. Awkward. So I decide not to fight any battles, especially those of Goliath proportions.

But You? You march right in and fight those battles for me. I stand in awe and watch as You take out my enemies one after the other. You make it look so easy!

Worry. . .gone! Anger. . .poof! Relationship problems. . . zapped in an instant!

You're an amazing warrior, Lord! I want to learn from how You fight. I want every victory to serve as a reminder that, even in the heat of war, I don't have to be afraid. Even when the enemy is staring me in the face, I can be at peace knowing that You're on my side.

Have I mentioned how grateful I am that You're on my side, Lord? I am! Amen.

As You Forgave Me

Instead, be kind to each other, tenderhearted,
forgiving one another, just as God
through Christ has forgiven you.

EPHESIANS 4:32 NLT

I've been falsely accused, Lord. Someone has blamed me for something I didn't do. (Ugh!) You're a God of justice, and I know You have my best interests at heart, but this is a tough one. How can I prove what they refuse to believe?

Today I'm asking You to go before me. I'm looking for justice. For truth. I want the real story to come out, not so I can hurt my accusers but so I can stand before others proven innocent.

I'll be honest. . .there's a part of me that wants to lash out at the accusers. The temptation is real. But I'm asking You to show me how to love them through this so that You can bring peace to all. I choose to be kind, tenderhearted, and forgiving even though their betrayal is cutting through my heart at this very moment.

You can fix this, Jesus! I'm believing for a miracle. I'm counting on You. I know You won't fail me. Amen.

Those Little Foxes

Catch for us the foxes, the little foxes that ruin
the vineyards, our vineyards that are in bloom.

SONG OF SONGS 2:15 NIV

I've heard this verse all my life, Jesus, about how the little foxes spoil the vine. I didn't understand it until recently—or think that it had anything to do with my life. Boy, does it!

Sometimes it really is the little things that get under my skin. They nag at me. They rob me of my peace. They irritate me! Those people with attitude. That one girl at school. That pop quiz in science class. My friend's snide comment. My mother's bad mood. Ugh. These little foxes add up, don't they? Before long, the whole vineyard is full!

Today, Lord, I give You the little foxes that have been sneaking in to steal my peace. I ask You to remove them permanently from my life. And if they do show up, Lord, help me not to overreact. I don't ever want to be robbed of my peace and joy. Amen.

Green Pastures

The Lord is my shepherd, I lack nothing.
He makes me lie down in green pastures,
he leads me beside quiet waters, he refreshes
my soul. He guides me along the right
paths for his name's sake.

PSALM 23:1–3 NIV

You make me lie down in green pastures. When I really think about those words, I'm reminded of the many times in my life when I had no choice but to stop, to spend time in Your presence, and to take a good look at what led me to that place.

Here's the thing I'm learning about green pastures, Jesus . . .they don't always look green at first. Sometimes when I'm forced to rest, to stop everything, I feel betrayed. I want to keep going. But the longer I rest in that place You've prepared, the more I see it for what it is: a gift.

You've got good pastures for me, fruitful and green. So when You bring me to a place of stillness, I won't argue. It's an honor to rest in green pastures with the One who knows me best and loves me most. Amen.

For Such a Time as This

*"For if you keep quiet at this time, help will come
to the Jews from another place. But you and your
father's house will be destroyed. Who knows if you
have not become queen for such a time as this?"*

ESTHER 4:14 NLV

Jesus, Your Word says that Esther became a queen "for such a time as this." You created her for the time she lived in. You timed her arrival on the scene perfectly. If she hadn't come into her position when she did, the Jewish people would have been wiped out. (Wow!)

You timed *my* arrival perfectly too. You have great things planned for me. I can trust Your plans and Your perfect timing. I was born in the right year, the right month, the right place, and the right situation to accomplish all that You have for me. What a remarkable thought!

I was born for such a time as this. Knowing that brings me incredible peace because I know the Author of my story. You can use me for good, Lord, just as You used Esther. I make myself available for that very thing! Amen.

You're Working It All for Good

And we know that God causes everything to work together for the good of those who love God and are called according to his purpose for them.

ROMANS 8:28 NLT

Everything. You promise to work everything for my good. Here's a question, Jesus: The things that steal my peace and my joy. . .those things too? You're going to use those and turn them into something beautiful? Oh, I hope so! Because right now they just feel impossible.

Money problems, relationship issues, my parents' broken marriage. . .how can You turn any of that to good, Lord? I just don't get how You can use those things.

And yet, You do. You use them to teach us how to handle things better next time. You grow us into the people we're supposed to be, in part because of our mess-ups, our mistakes.

You'll work it all for good. And I'm guessing there will be plenty of lessons learned along the way. Thank You for turning our ashes into something beautiful, Lord! Amen.

My Treasure Is in You

"But store up for yourselves treasures in heaven, where moths and vermin do not destroy, and where thieves do not break in and steal. For where your treasure is, there your heart will be also."

MATTHEW 6:20–21 NIV

Jesus, I can imagine myself opening a real treasure box and peeking inside. What will I see? Rubies? Diamonds? Emeralds? I'm picturing the shimmer and shine now.

You've told me that wherever my treasure is, there my heart will be also. So I don't want to sell myself short! I will seek You, for You are far greater than any jewels I can imagine. Your value is above and beyond anything I have ever seen with human eyes. And I know I can trust You, so I will place my heart in Your very capable hands.

I love that You see me as a treasure too. When You open the jewelry box of my heart, You see plenty of shimmer and shine because You're looking at a reflection of Yourself. You are my great treasure and my ultimate reward, Jesus. I love You! I can't wait to spend eternity getting to know You more. Amen.

Peace, a Lovely Fruit

*But the fruit of the Spirit is love, joy, peace,
patience, kindness, goodness, faithfulness, gentleness,
self-control; against such things there is no law.*

GALATIANS 5:22–23 ESV

You've given me so many fruits of the Spirit, Jesus. I see them all listed in today's verses, and I can't help but smile. They are mine to enjoy and mine to share with others. (I'm very generous, I promise! Sharing comes naturally to me.)

One of the main fruits is peace. What good would it do to have joy, faithfulness, goodness, self-control, or any of the others if there was no peace in my heart? Peace is like the glue that holds it all together! I love how all the gifts work together in tandem. One operates best with the others. You truly think of everything, Jesus!

So today I want to slow down long enough to thank You for the gift of Your great peace. It's one fruit I would never want to be without. I'm so grateful it's mine for the picking, in good seasons and bad. Amen.

One Is Not the Other

*What sorrow for those who say that evil is good
and good is evil, that dark is light and light is
dark, that bitter is sweet and sweet is bitter.*

ISAIAH 5:20 NLT

It drives me crazy, Jesus! Just a few minutes on social media, and I'm ready to pull my hair out. So many people are calling evil good and good evil. When did this happen?

I can remember a time in my life when truth was truth, and no one was afraid to speak it, Lord. Don't they know? Don't they see that wandering from Your truth will lead to destruction instead of peace? The world is so lost, and I wonder if things are just going to get worse.

Help me to be a light and to spread the message of truth— that good is *not* evil and evil is *not* good. I need to speak the truth, the whole truth, and nothing but the truth.

But I need to do it with love.

Oh, help!

I want to reflect all that truly is good so that others will be won to You. Amen.

Mansions Untold

*"In my Father's house are many rooms.
If it were not so, would I have told you
that I go to prepare a place for you?"*

JOHN 14:2 ESV

No house hunting for me, Jesus! Why would I keep searching when I've already found the most beautiful home of all, right inside Your heart?

Now that I have experienced every room, every square inch of Your holy space, why would I wander off? Nothing can compare. (Can I just say that You're a master decorator? You've taken the time to fill each room with such precious things, and all for my enjoyment! Lord, You truly thought of everything.)

And to think, this is just a sample of all the days to come in heaven, where You are even now preparing mansions untold. I will dwell in Your house forever, Lord. Wow! Now that's a home that's well built! You are the Master Builder. I can't wait to live with You forever! Amen.

Well Rested

The sleep of a laborer is sweet, whether they
eat little or much, but as for the rich, their
abundance permits them no sleep.

ECCLESIASTES 5:12 NIV

A good night's sleep works wonders, Jesus! I always feel so much better after I am well rested. Snuggling under the covers, hugging that pillow, drifting off into a peaceful state . . .I love it!

I'm so glad You created our bodies to need downtime. That's one reason I love today's verse so much. You actually created me to need and crave sleep. You knew that dreamy half-awake, half-asleep feeling would be like gold to me.

Sure, You've given me a lot of work to do each day, but that dozing-off feeling is my reward. It's Your way of saying, *"Job well done, kid!"*

I never want to get so caught up with busyness that I don't take the time to rest. No out-of-balance living for this girl! Thanks for helping me with this. Amen.

You Hold Nothing Back

For the LORD God is our sun and our shield.
He gives us grace and glory. The LORD will withhold
no good thing from those who do what is right.

PSALM 84:11 NLT

Sugar in my tea, Lord. It makes all the difference. Sweetens things up. The same is true when I allow Your peace to take over my heart. What once tasted bitter is now sweet and good.

You're a God of sugar and spice. You've got lots of pleasures in store for me. I love this verse because it says that You pour out good things on those who do what is right.

Now, I'm not saying I'm going to do right just so I can have the goodies, Lord. But it does make me smile that Your goodness is poured out when I walk in obedience.

I'll obey You because I love You. And because You love me, You'll continue to pour out blessings that go above anything I could ask or think.

You hold nothing back from me. I will hold nothing back from You. Thank You for Your abundance! Amen.

An Untroubled Heart

Jesus said to his disciples, "Don't be worried!
Have faith in God and have faith in me."

JOHN 14:1 CEV

If I praise You in the dark, I know You will bring me into the light. This is Your pattern for peace, even during the most difficult times. When someone I love is near death. When a friend has rejected me. When I feel like I'm not smart enough or pretty enough or popular enough. When my heart is broken in two. I will choose to praise You, even in the dark. When my family is going through a tough season. When I'm not feeling well. When I'm upset at a teacher who treated me unfairly. Even then, I will do my best not to let my heart be troubled. I'll go right on praising, in the very middle of the dark spaces.

You are the Author of light, and I will praise until I see sunlight again. I've learned—sometimes the hard way—that it really is possible to praise my way through, Lord. So that's my plan, no matter how dark things get. Amen.

Before I Was Formed

"Before I formed you in the womb I knew you,
and before you were born I consecrated you;
I appointed you a prophet to the nations."

Before You formed me, You knew me! The prophet Jeremiah realized this great truth. Before he ever came on the scene, You knew all about him, Lord—who he would reach, what he would say, where he would live. . .everything.

It's remarkable to think that You know all of that about me too. You took the time to craft me in my mother's womb, carefully detailing every little part that makes me, me! I'm unique because You designed me that way.

But even before that, You loved me! Before You spun any of my cells into place. Before anyone ever saw my freckles or chubby thighs. You loved me when I was just a twinkle in my mama's eye. There's nothing in my life that You are unaware of. You love me deeply! You always have. That gives me a tremendous sense of peace, knowing that my Creator was on the job long before I was around. Amen.

114

No Pretending with You

*"All those the Father gives me will come to me,
and whoever comes to me I will never drive away."*

JOHN 6:37 NIV

Sometimes I feel like the great pretender, Jesus. I'm not my truest self when I'm around others. I want them to like me, to admire me. So I try extra hard to fit in.

Then there are other times when I hide away so I don't have to try at all. On those days, it's easier not to bother. They won't accept me anyway. At least, that's my fear. (Just keeping it real.)

It's hard to just relax and be myself sometimes. Why do I even worry about what others think about me? Why am I so concerned that I won't fit in?

What good news, to know that I can always fit in with You. I don't even have to try! With You, I can just be who You created me to be. I will come to You, and You will never turn me away—even when I'm my truest self. I'm so grateful, Jesus! Thank You! Amen.

Confusion, Be Gone!

For God is not a God of confusion but of peace.

1 CORINTHIANS 14:33 ESV

"Should I move forward or stay here, Jesus? Should I turn right or left? Which voice should I listen to? Everything in my life seems so confusing! Ugh!" How often have I spoken those words? Crazy situations come, and they bring confusion with them. I get turned around. Lost. I'm convinced I'll never find a way out, so I get stuck.

But You? You're not a God of confusion. In fact, if I'm confused, I can be sure it's the enemy of my soul trying to trip me up! I won't let him though. I'm onto his tricks. You are a God of peace, not chaos. So when this whirling, swirling world threatens to knock me off my game, I will stand firm, look the enemy in the eye, and say, "Not today, devil!"

Thank You for giving me the wisdom to realize that You will never confuse me, Father! Amen.

I Will Keep Your Statutes

*Blessed are those who keep his statutes
and seek him with all their heart.*

PSALM 119:2 NIV

I guess it goes without saying that I haven't always been a rule follower, Lord. Many times, I made up my own rules as I went along. Whatever felt right to me in the moment was what I did.

And there were consequences, of course. Oh boy, were there consequences. Some of them I'm still living out.

Oh, but now things are different! I love You. I love Your Word. And I'm so fascinated by Your way of living that I want to follow You all the days of my life. I can find true peace in living this way, Lord. That promise is in today's verse: Blessed are those who keep Your statutes and seek You with all their heart.

I will follow hard after You and be blessed! Amen.

Faith Comes by Hearing

So faith comes from hearing,
and hearing through the word of Christ.

ROMANS 10:17 ESV

How will people know unless I tell them? That's the big question, Jesus. I'm not always bold when I'm face-to-face with people, especially those who disagree with me. I get nervous. I wonder what they will think of me. These days, with so much persecution of Christians going on, I even get a little nervous that I will be attacked. Or canceled, as social media calls it. Will people walk away if I offend them with truth?

But I have no choice! I have to speak the truth. You tell me in Your Word that faith comes by hearing, and hearing by the Word of God. Your Word contains *only* truth. I have to speak up in order for others to know. I want them to have the peace, confidence, and joy that I have. And I want them to spend eternity in heaven with me.

Give me courage to speak up, I pray. I will speak the truth in love. Amen.

By Your Own Mercy

*He saved us, not because of the righteous
things we had done, but because of his mercy.
He washed away our sins, giving us a new
birth and new life through the Holy Spirit.*

TITUS 3:5 NLT

You've welcomed me into Your throne room, Jesus. I don't have to be afraid. I don't have to be ashamed, no matter how messed up I am or how many mess-ups I've made. You say, *"Come on in, kiddo. Sit with Me, eat with Me, be with Me."* The King of all kings wants me to sit at His feet. The Lord of all lords wants to spend time with me, His child. I'm so blessed!

Jesus, this is all because of Your great mercy. You didn't save me because of my righteousness. (Whew!) You saved me, washed me, gave me a fresh chance. Why? Because of Your great mercy!

I know I'll probably make more mistakes. But I also know that I can count on You to be merciful when I ask for forgiveness. Thank You for that amazing mercy and grace, Lord! Amen.

Wings of a Dove

I said, "Oh, that I had the wings of a dove!
I would fly away and be at rest."

PSALM 55:6 NIV

There have been so many situations in my life, Jesus, when I wanted to run away. I wanted to pack my bags and take off to a place where life was easier, where arguments didn't exist, where hard things didn't take place.

Like the man who wrote this psalm, I would love to fly away. If only I had the wings of a dove, then I could be at rest. I can almost picture myself soaring through the clouds, looking down on the problems below. Bye-bye, chaos! Bye-bye, confusion! I'm up here, living in peace!

Oh, but here's the good news I have discovered. When I walk with You, Your peace transcends the turmoil. It transcends the traumas and the anxieties. I truly am a dove at flight as long as You hold my heart in Your hands. I can rise above it all, Lord, with Your help. Amen.

Undivided

Teach me to follow you, and I will obey
your truth. Always keep me faithful.

PSALM 86:11 CEV

I am so easily distracted by bright and shiny objects, Jesus! Sometimes I forget to be faithful to You because I get caught off guard by the treasures of this world and all the things that I think it can offer me. They dazzle! They delight! They call my name!

Not for long, though. I'm learning that true satisfaction does not come from the things I think I want or need, even the bright and shiny ones. They are illusions, a trick of the enemy to divide my heart and pull me from You. The only real satisfaction comes from time with You and in Your Word.

I need to stay focused, Jesus! I need an undivided heart, one that is completely devoted to You. No distractions. No temptations. Only You, Jesus. Nothing can ever compare to You, and certainly nothing can bring peace as You do. Give me an undivided heart, I pray. Amen.

In the End

*Their hearts are secure, they will have no fear;
in the end they will look in triumph on their foes.*

PSALM 112:8 NIV

Things don't always go the way I think they will, Jesus. Sometimes I'm sure of how something will turn out, but then circumstances don't go my way. Ugh! Friends fight. I fail a test. My best friend moves away. A grandparent dies. And I wonder: Where were You, Lord? Did You take a vacation? Don't You care?

Then time passes. Days go by, or weeks or months. . .and suddenly all is made clear. You give me perspective. And perspective brings great peace. In the end, all things work together for my good.

Help me learn to trust *before* the end of the story comes into view, Jesus! I want to trust You fully. I want to walk in peace from start to finish with no doubts. Amen.

Committed to You

Commit your work to the Lord,
and your plans will be established.

PROVERBS 16:3 ESV

I've made up my mind. I'm committed. I'm not going to tell You one thing today, Jesus, and change my mind tomorrow. I'm in this for the long haul. I'm committed to You, to this life You've called me to, and to the tasks You place in front of me, no matter how difficult they might feel in the moment. I have peace when I trust in You! I'm watching Your plans unfold in my life even now. (How exciting!) They will be established in Your timing and Your way.

I know the enemy of my soul is hard at work trying to discourage me. I won't let him. Any pain I experience along the way will be worth it in the end, as Your plans come to pass. I'm going to have a great time watching You work, Jesus! Amen.

Too Heavy a Weight

Therefore, since we are surrounded by so great a cloud of witnesses, let us also lay aside every weight, and sin which clings so closely, and let us run with endurance the race that is set before us.

HEBREWS 12:1 ESV

Remember that heavy box I picked up the other day, Jesus? It weighed w-a-y too much, but I was sure I could handle it without any help. So I did. . .and paid a heavy price later on with a sore back and shoulders.

Some burdens were never mine to carry. I picked them up needlessly when I should have left them in Your trustworthy hands. I often wonder why my peace is gone and my strength is zapped. I end up hunched over, racked with pain (emotional, spiritual, and physical), but it's because I lifted something far too heavy for me.

Thank You for the reminder that I was never meant to carry it all. Your Word tells me to lay aside every weight, not pick them up! Next time I'm about to reach for something that I'm not meant to lift, stop me, I pray. Amen.

A Day Off

On the seventh day God ended His work which He had done. And He rested on the seventh day from all His work which He had done. Then God honored the seventh day and made it holy, because in it He rested from all His work which He had done.

GENESIS 2:2–3 NLV

I need a day off, Jesus! After reading the story of creation, I see that You did too! That's why You rested on the seventh day, and You want me to rest too. I don't have to feel guilty about giving my body, soul, and spirit time to refresh. I learned from You that a Sabbath rest is critical for my survival.

Today's scripture shows me that You worked, worked, worked. For six days, You performed miracle after miracle. The things I do pale in comparison to Your marvelous, creative work, but there are weeks when I feel like I've been moving heaven and earth to get things done. Then I get to that seventh day, and I'm beat! I'm worn out!

So I'll do what You did, Lord. I'll rest. I'll make a point to say no to the things I need to turn down for the sake of my physical health and my spirit. Thank You for leading by example, Lord. My body thanks You. Amen.

None but You

Whom have I in heaven but you?
And earth has nothing I desire besides you.
My flesh and my heart may fail, but God is the
strength of my heart and my portion forever.

PSALM 73:25–26 NIV

There's a lot of confusion in this world, Lord. It's hard to know what we can believe. Can we put our trust in the media? Can we put our trust in politicians? Can we put our trust in friends or family members? I don't think so! They let us down, time and time again.

The only One who has fully earned my trust is You, Jesus! I won't ever have to doubt Your Word. It never changes. It's as real and as perfect today as it was thousands of years ago. (That's a real miracle!)

My heart can be so peaceful when I put my trust in You alone. (Ahh! That feels good!) There's nothing I need or want besides You! What a trustworthy God You are! Amen.

Packing My Bags with Peace

Lying is in the heart of those who plan what is bad,
but those who plan peace have joy.

PROVERBS 12:20 NLV

Some people seem to love chaos and pain. They thrive on it, or so it seems! These people enjoy causing pain in others, which is tough to watch, especially when people I love are being hurt.

I've never understood this sort of cruelty, Jesus. That's because You have called me to something completely different. You would never counsel me to scheme against another person or to hurt anyone else. It's not in Your nature, and it shouldn't be in mine either!

I'm following Your lead and planning for something much better: peace. I am packing it in my bags and taking it with me everywhere I go. It's not heavy. In fact, it's almost like carrying nothing at all! When I live like this, I won't hurt others along the way, and I won't hurt myself. Thanks for the kind of peace that leads to true joy. Amen.

In Spirit and in Truth

*"But the time is coming—indeed it's here now—
when true worshipers will worship the Father
in spirit and in truth. The Father is looking for
those who will worship him that way."*

JOHN 4:23 NLT

We have our routines, Lord. Sometimes, we can get stuck in
a rut even in the way we worship. I confess that sometimes
my prayer time with You isn't as great as it should be. I just
mumble the same words over and over, hoping that's enough.
Sometimes my Bible reading time seems dull too, as if my
heart isn't in it. (Is that awful to confess?)

But You, Lord? You can come on the scene and with one
word change everything! You literally transform me when
I take the time to worship in spirit and in truth. It's not just
head knowledge I need; it's heart knowledge. It's Holy Spirit
knowledge! And if I just ask, all of that can be mine as I spend
time daily with You. So today I open my heart to the flow of
Your Spirit so that I can have a life-changing encounter with
You. Amen.

All You Created Is Good

*Since everything God created is good, we should
not reject any of it but receive it with thanks.*

1 TIMOTHY 4:4 NLT

I can't think of one so-so thing that You ever created, Jesus. Every single creation is spectacular, every one! From fluffy clouds floating in the sky above me to teensy-tiny grasshoppers hopping through the grass under my feet. From the smile on a toddler's face to the wagging tail of my favorite dog. From a juicy clementine to the tart flavor of a raspberry. You thought of literally everything!

So when I think of how You took the time to create me, I have to admit. . .I'm not so-so either. You gave me a unique voice, my own skin tone, my quirky (sometimes crazy!) personality, and special gifts and abilities, some of which I'm just discovering or developing. Instead of cutting myself down or worrying about how I don't measure up, I'll remember who made me. I was created by the Master Designer! All You created is good, Lord. . .even me! Amen.

Upright in Heart

Keep on giving Your loving-kindness
to those who know You. Keep on being
right and good to the pure in heart.

PSALM 36:10 NLV

It's one thing to follow the rules for the sake of following the rules. It's another thing altogether to obey because I know it will please Your heart and bring You joy, Lord.

Your Word says that You will continue to give Your love to those who know You and that You will pour out Your righteousness to those who are upright in heart. You know what this shows me? You're checking my motivations. Oh my!

If I want to have real peace, real joy, then I must live this way. No showing off. No pretending. No bluffing or acting like I've got it together when I'm really a mess on the inside. I don't fool anyone when I act like this, anyway. . . especially You.

I want to be upright through and through, but I'll definitely need Your help, Lord. Help me be upright in heart. Amen.

Because I Trust in You

*You will keep in perfect peace all who trust in you,
all whose thoughts are fixed on you!*

ISAIAH 26:3 NLT

I will keep walking, Jesus! It's not always easy to keep going, but I won't stop. When I'm faced with a fuzzy view, when I'm not sure what's ahead of me, I'm tempted to come to a grinding halt, to let fear lock me up. That's just what the enemy wants. But I'm on to his tricks! I will keep moving. I will not allow fear to freeze me in place anymore. I will not get stuck. I will move forward in peace that only You can bring.

I'm learning that there's only one way to keep on trusting, and that's by keeping my thoughts on You, Lord. They want to go a thousand different directions, but I'll focus them squarely on You, where they belong. When I do that, my mind is fixed. My heart is in perfect peace. My trust is fully and completely restored. Thank You for that! Amen.

Walking Humbly with You

*O man, He has told you what is good. What does the
Lord ask of you but to do what is fair and to love
kindness, and to walk without pride with your God?*

MICAH 6:8 NLV

Sometimes my pride gets the best of me, Jesus. I get a little too puffed up. I think too much of my own needs or my own image. I forget that You have called me to lay down my pride. When I get like this, all peace is gone. My eyes are too focused on myself. (When did I become so obsessed with myself anyway?)

Today I choose to lay down my pride. I will look to You, not myself! Today's verse says that You require me to walk without pride. You've also called me to do what is right and to love mercy. These are requirements. But none of these things are possible when I'm hyperfocused on me, myself, and I.

I want to walk with You, laying down "self" in the process. But I'm going to need Your help, Lord. Guard my heart, I pray. Amen.

Your Goodness and Mercy

Surely goodness and mercy shall follow
me all the days of my life: and I will dwell
in the house of the LORD for ever.

PSALM 23:6 KJV

Your Word promises me that goodness and mercy will follow me all the days of my life. I can see them, hear them, even feel them chasing after me!

Why should I worry about tomorrow when goodness and mercy have promised to go all the way with me? Why should I be afraid of the battles I face when goodness and mercy walk onto the battleground with me? Why would I ever feel alone when You're right there, offering me the best of Yourself?

I can chill, knowing You've got me covered, Jesus! You care so much, and You are so good to me. It makes me smile when I think that You will chase me down with Your goodness and mercy all the days of my life and that I can dwell—live—in Your house forever. This is such happy news! Thank You, thank You! Amen.

The Work of Your Hands

*For You have made me glad by what You have
done, O Lord. I will sing for joy at the works
of Your hands. How great are Your works,
O Lord! How deep are Your thoughts!*

PSALM 92:4–5 NLV

How many worlds have You created, Jesus? In this amazing universe, how many planets exist because You spun them into existence? How many stars did You hang in the sky so that You could use them to reflect Your glory? When I start to think about it all, my mind is in a whirl. I'm boggled by Your vastness, Your greatness, and Your creativity!

When I think of all these things, I have to wonder how Your mind works. Is it like ten million of the finest computers working together, Jesus, with a little bit of Michelangelo and Rembrandt tossed in?

Your ways are too deep for me! Your thoughts are too high. But I will stand in awe as I consider Your great works, remembering that You cared enough to create me too. Amen.

Even Then. . .

Even if an army gathers against me,
my heart will not be afraid. Even if war
rises against me, I will be sure of You.

PSALM 27:3 NLV

You are the risen King, Jesus! You overcame death, hell, and the grave. As You hung on the cross, an army gathered against You—Satan and his minions were ready to take You down. (Little did they know!) The war of the ages was waged against You. But You overcame! You walked out of that tomb three days later, alive and well.

Why would I ever doubt that You will come through for me? That You will not only see but actually fix the tough situations I find myself in? I can rest easy, knowing that the One who walked out of the tomb is in complete control of my life. Battles will be waged against me. I see what the enemy of my soul is up to. But I'm a daughter of the King! Placing my trust in a risen Savior like You brings great peace! Amen.

My Hard Heart

"And I will give you a new heart, and a new spirit I will put within you. And I will remove the heart of stone from your flesh and give you a heart of flesh."

EZEKIEL 36:26 ESV

Sometimes I feel You're like a farmer, breaking up the ground of my hard heart, Lord. You're chopping up all the hard places, making room for tiny seedlings to be planted. Seedlings of hope. Seedlings of joy. Seedlings of peace, of trust.

The process isn't always easy. I've experienced pain as You've dug out some of the nastiness in the soil of my heart. (Ick!) But it's for my good. It's for my peace. It's for a healthy crop to rise from that soil next time around and for my hard heart to be softened.

So do Your work, even though it might seem painful in the moment. I know that a beautiful crop is coming, so I will trust You with the planting process. I will also trust that the God of peace can calm and soften my heart in the meantime.

Thank You, Father! Amen.

My Hope Comes from You

Yes, my soul, find rest in God;
my hope comes from him.

PSALM 62:5 NIV

Hope is everywhere. I can see it in the eyes of a child. I notice it in an elderly woman's smile as she delivers cookies to a neighbor. I see hope in the hearts of my parents as they work hard to provide for our family. I witness it in the face of a cancer patient as she undergoes chemotherapy.

Hope is a priceless thing, Jesus, and I can only get it from You. Nothing this world has to offer can compare. I know because I've searched for it on my own. I tried to find hope in my schoolwork, in my activities. It failed me. I looked for it in my relationships, but those people weren't You, Lord. (Perfection? Far from it!)

I now know that only You can bring hope. And when You do, You usher in blissful peace to walk alongside it. That's how I choose to live from now on! Amen.

You Will Make a Way

No temptation has overtaken you that is not common to man. God is faithful, and he will not let you be tempted beyond your ability, but with the temptation he will also provide the way of escape, that you may be able to endure it.

1 CORINTHIANS 10:13 ESV

You make a way where there seems to be no way, Jesus! I've faced dead end after dead end in my life. There were situations that felt impossible. I just knew I wasn't going to make it through. But somehow, You plowed right through those awkward situations and made a superhighway right down the middle!

Because You have made a way in the past, I can trust You with my present and my future. (Thank You for that!) The situations in front of me are so confusing! I have no idea how You're going to work this out. But this much I do know: You can carve out a path in the desert and make a way through the wilderness. The road will be paved with hope, peace, joy, and courage, and I will travel it hand in hand with You. It brings me so much peace to know You're my Way Maker. Amen.

Shine, Jesus. . .Shine!

Light shines on the righteous and
joy on the upright in heart.

PSALM 97:11 NIV

There are spooky dark shadows that try to drown out the daylight at times, Jesus. They scare me, if I'm being honest. My hands shake and my knees knock when I'm not able to see what's in front of me. I'm scared I'll end up getting hurt. But You've opened my eyes to something amazing! There's no such thing as darkness as long as I stick close to You. I see those sneaky shadows for what they really are—illusions, a trick of the enemy to try to stop me from moving forward . . .a tool to steal my peace.

I won't be fooled, not even for a moment. You are the God of light! You're like a superbright flashlight guiding my way. You know what's coming around the bend, and You are my radiant Savior, taking hold of my hand and leading me past the shadows! I'll enter Your glorious presence, where everything will be revealed.

No more knocking knees for me, Lord! Shine, Jesus. . . shine! Amen.

I Pour Out My Heart

Trust in Him at all times, O people. Pour out your heart before Him. God is a safe place for us.

PSALM 62:8 NLV

Mask up, they say! Put on that mask to protect yourself from illness. I'm sure hoping it does the trick, Jesus, because I'd like to stay healthy! But as I think about that mask, I'm reminded of another one that I hardly ever talk about. There are times when I feel like I've masked my heart. I've kept areas of it hidden away from people I love, from You, and even from myself. I'm afraid to go there because it might hurt too much.

Today I choose to pull off that heart mask and reveal everything to You—the good, the bad, and the ugly. I know You won't be shocked. You already know what's hiding in there, after all! But I also know that I can trust You to heal my heart when I truly reveal what's inside. So enough with the cover-up! Have Your way in my heart, I pray. Change me from the inside out. Unmask me, Jesus! Amen.

I'm Listening, Lord

Pay close attention! Come to me and live.
I will promise you the eternal love and
loyalty that I promised David.

ISAIAH 55:3 CEV

This is a noisy world, Jesus! The girls I hang out with, TVs, phones. These are just a few of the things demanding my time and attention. My teacher's voice, my mom telling me to clean my room, my favorite song on the radio. These are other things I hear.

Sometimes I'm so busy listening to everything the world has to offer that I forget to listen when You speak. Today's verse reminds me what to do. I have to come into Your presence, but that's not enough. There are really specific (cool!) things You want to speak to my heart. That means I have to tune out the other stuff in order to really hear Your voice.

You speak life! If I don't listen, I'm going to miss out on something really important! So I'm leaning in today. I'll shush those other voices and listen only to You. Speak to me, Lord. I'm listening! Amen.

Cleansed and Set Free!

*If we confess our sins, he is faithful
and just to forgive us our sins and to
cleanse us from all unrighteousness.*

1 JOHN 1:9 ESV

Why do I keep messing things up, Lord? My heart's in the right place. But I'm so forgetful. I promise to do things, and then they slip my mind. I make things harder on others when I make mistakes.

So many times, I've been caught in the enemy's trap. He convinces me there's no way forward.

But You've set me free, Lord! You said in Your Word that if I confess my sins, You would be faithful and just to forgive me. You also said that You would wipe away all my ickiness. My unrighteousness. Not a little. Not a tiny amount. All. You cleanse me from *all* the things I've ever done wrong.

Have You already covered my future mess-ups, Lord? I have a feeling I'm still far from perfect. But I'm resting easy, my heart filled with peace, because I get it now! You've already got me covered. Amen.

Mountain, Be Moved!

*Jesus told his disciples: Have faith in God!
If you have faith in God and don't doubt, you
can tell this mountain to get up and jump into
the sea, and it will. Everything you ask for in
prayer will be yours, if you only have faith.*

MARK 11:22–24 CEV

I have faced so many scary mountains on my faith journey, Jesus. I marched all the way around many of them. I did my best to climb some of them. And there were many that I wished I could tunnel through.

But You, Lord? You keep reminding me that all I have to do is *speak* a word to the mountains in front of me, and they will be gone, just like that. Poof! Mountain no more! And when that mountain disappears, peace washes over me like a river. Now that I see Your greatness, now that my faith is stronger, I don't think I'll wait for the mountains to move to start praising You. Even when they loom large in front of me, I'll sing a song of praise. I'll imagine how different the road ahead will look once it's flattened.

So get ready, mountains! I'm coming for you! With only a word, you're going down! Amen.

Bigger Than My Problems

I will give thanks to you, LORD, with all my heart;
I will tell of all your wonderful deeds.

Sometimes, my problems seem bigger than You, Jesus. That's a terrible thing to confess, I guess, but in those moments when I'm facing something of Goliath proportions, I forget that You are bigger. My peace goes right out the window! (Where's that faith I keep bragging about? Can't I manage even a teensy-tiny bit when Goliath stands in front of me?)

Here's the truth: You *are* greater, and You can, in one instant, flatten those giants to the ground! You don't even need a slingshot and five stones like David. With just a word from You, down they go!

So why should I be afraid? Who cares if the problems are big, when I've placed my trust in the One who is above all? You are greater, Lord. What peace I can have! You will win these battles without even flinching. Thanks for that reminder. It brings me so much peace! Amen.

I Glory in Your Name!

Glory in his holy name; let the hearts
of those who seek the LORD rejoice.

PSALM 105:3 NIV

Life is a celebration, Jesus! I have so much to be grateful for. When I look at the amazing blessings You've poured out in my life, when I really pause to think about the journey You've brought me on and all the times You've set me free, placed my feet on solid ground. . .it makes me want to throw a party! Woo-hoo!

I'm already thinking of the invitation list. I'll invite all those friends who thought You wouldn't come through for me. They need to see that You are faithful. I'll also invite those who need a faith boost, like the friend going through cancer and my grandmother who's feeling alone.

I have a lot of peace today, not in spite of the struggles I've been through but because of them. Because I have struggled and overcome, I have reason to celebrate! What a party I'm going to throw! Amen.

Into Your Marvelous Light

But you are a chosen group of people. You are
the King's religious leaders. You are a holy
nation. You belong to God. He has done this for
you so you can tell others how God has called
you out of darkness into His great light.

1 PETER 2:9 NLV

I'm worried about a friend, Jesus. You know the one. She's acting weird. Something's off. I feel like she's deliberately pulling away, like she's afraid to move forward. Maybe she's not sure of what the future holds. Show me how to help her through this. Please? Bring peace to her heart. Give her the freedom to trust You with what she is facing. It's a big deal to her, and that makes it a big deal to me too! She's got some huge struggles in her life.

The Bible says we're a chosen race, a royal priesthood, a holy nation. You've said that we are a people of Your own possession. My friend needs this reminder! Today's verse also says that You've called us out of darkness into Your great, bright light. She needs that so much! Should I be the one to tell her? Give me the words, I pray, and the perfect opportunity to share some hope with my friend. Amen.

A Gentle Father

Give thanks to the Lord, for he is good!
His faithful love endures forever.

PSALM 107:1 NLT

This puppy You gave me to love and take care of is a lot of work, Jesus! He chews my shoes, has accidents, and is eating us out of house and home! And boy, can he run from me when he slips out of his leash! The neighbors have seen me running down the street. I'm sure it made them laugh! Still, I wouldn't trade him for anything in the world. He's my bundle of joy, and (naughty or not) I love him.

I wonder if You feel like that about me sometimes. Am I a handful? Do You have to chase me down? I've slipped away from You lots of times as I made a mad dash toward dangerous circumstances, but You always caught me, Lord!

I'm so grateful You are a gentle, loving Father, so patient with me even when I'm a piece of work! Today's verse promises that You will be faithful to me no matter how naughty I am. Your love endures forever. Thank You for the gentle way You love, Lord! Amen.

I Will Rest Secure

*And so my heart is glad. My soul is full of
joy. My body also will rest without fear.*

PSALM 16:9 NLV

I get so tensed up sometimes, Lord. I can feel it in my neck and shoulders. All that tension gives me headaches, makes me snippy with others, and is probably bad for my health too! I love that Your Word says my body can rest secure. When I put my trust in You, my shoulders relax, my neck doesn't kink, and headaches fade away. I feel peace in my whole body when I'm in a more relaxed state of mind. Ahh! What a relief!

So I'll lift up a song of praise! My heart will be glad, and my tongue will rejoice. I'll experience the benefits in this body of mine, just like You promised.

Your ways really are best, Lord. They bring peace to my soul and health to my weary body! Thank You for teaching me how to rest easy in You. Amen.

Evident to All

*Let your gentleness be evident
to all. The Lord is near.*

PHILIPPIANS 4:5 NIV

I don't want to be that person who treats others badly, Jesus! When people look at me, when my friends hang out with me, I want them to walk away from the experience feeling more peaceful, more loved, and more encouraged.

Today's verse says that my gentleness should be evident to all, and that includes my family at home and the people in my inner circle, although sometimes they're the ones I'm the most short tempered with!) But they're watching. Oh boy, are they watching! And they need to see Your love, Your peace, and Your joy shining through me as I speak gently and lovingly to them, even when the situation is t-o-u-g-h!

Guard my words, please! Let it be obvious to everyone that Your love, Your peace, and Your joy live deep in my heart. I hope when they hang out with me that they leave feeling encouraged and stronger. I want to lead by example, Lord! Amen.

You're Not Changing

*"For I the LORD do not change; therefore you,
O children of Jacob, are not consumed."*

MALACHI 3:6 ESV

I remember how, as a little kid, I used to love to change clothes. I would get dressed for the day and then switch to something else. When I got bored with that outfit, I would put on another. Then I would turn to my dress-up clothes, my costumes, and even my mom's clothes.

I had a blast taking off one outfit and putting on another. Okay, sure. . .I left a big mess on those days. I can still remember being scolded by Mom, who made me pick it all up when I was done.

You're not like me, Jesus. You leave behind zero messes. If You were always changing like me, the world would be in chaos! But You? You never change! You show up to each new day dressed in righteousness, peace, and joy. Year in and year out, You're the same. And You're teaching me that I can follow Your lead. Help me be consistent like You, Jesus! Amen.

Light to My Eyes

*The Laws of the Lord are right,
giving joy to the heart. The Word of the
Lord is pure, giving light to the eyes.*

PSALM 19:8 NLV

Sometimes I can't see the things that are right in front of me, Jesus. I open the refrigerator door looking for the orange juice, and I just don't see it. Then I figure out it was on the shelf right in front of me. W-w-what?! How is this possible?

The same thing happens sometimes when I read the Bible. I don't always get the full meaning of a verse. But then, at just the right moment, You shed Your light, and that verse jumps to life in my heart. I get it! I really, truly get it.

Today's verse reminds me that Your laws are supposed to do that—bring joy to my heart. Your commands are an amazing light (bright as the noonday sun!) and they show me which way to go. When I follow hard after You, there will always be light to guide the way. Thank You, God, for giving light to my eyes! Amen.

Make Music with My Soul

My heart will not be moved, O God. I will sing.
Yes, I will sing praises with my soul.

PSALM 108:1 NLV

You've given me a happy heart, Jesus! All day long this joyful heart of mine is ready to break into song. You've given me so much to celebrate!

I wasn't always this way. I can remember a time when my heart was broken. It was anything but happy. The only song on my heart back then was "Woe is me! How terrible my life is!" On and on I went, singing the depressing tune. (Sorry about that!)

But You changed all of that! When You stepped in and gave me the kind of peace that only You can offer, my whole way of thinking changed. My heart was transformed! So I will do as today's verse suggests: I'll sing. I'll make music with my soul. And I'll do it all because my heart is filled with peace from You. Thank You, Jesus, for the power to change! Amen.

You Straighten My Path

In all your ways submit to him,
and he will make your paths straight.

PROVERBS 3:6 NIV

I've headed down many crooked paths in my life, Jesus. They brought me nothing but confusion and chaos. When that happens, I get twisted up and can't figure out which way to go. But You? You lead me down a straight path. It's a narrow one (for sure!), but You make my vision clear and bright with every step I take. I can step forward with confidence and peace in my heart, knowing that when I do things Your way, the path in front of me will become more obvious with every step. (Well, hello there, road! I see you now!)

Thank You for caring so much about my journey, Jesus! Thanks for taking the time to straighten things out when they're lopsided or crooked. (I've given You plenty of opportunities, haven't I, Lord?) You love me anyway, and I'm so grateful. Amen.

You Teach Me in the Night

*I praise you, L*ORD*, for being my guide. Even in the darkest night, your teachings fill my mind.*

PSALM 16:7 CEV

You've given wisdom to lots of people, Jesus. I've trusted in a lot of them over the years. Their advice helps when I'm stuck and don't know which way to go. They come along and give me their ideas, their perspective, and suddenly I know what to do. I definitely need godly counsel from time to time.

But I'm learning that You, Jesus, are the greatest counselor of all. You don't charge overtime when I come to You after hours. Even in the middle of the night, You are right there. Your Spirit advises me, speaks to me, and whispers direction, wisdom, guidance, and peace.

So, I will praise You, my Wonderful Counselor! Even in the wee hours of the night, I'll count on You above all others. (They're probably grateful I'm not calling them at that time of day, anyway.) I love Your advice, Jesus! Amen.

Your Breath, Your Spirit

*"But it is the spirit in a person, the breath of the
Almighty, that gives them understanding."*

JOB 32:8 NIV

I just don't get it! How many times have I used those words in
my life? Way too many to count, Jesus. I don't always understand what's going on. But with the breath of Your Spirit, with
Your discernment, I can see things I couldn't see before. I
can hear things I couldn't hear before. And I can understand
things that made no sense to me before. (Wow!)

I've been wondering about all those people who have a
lot of book smarts but no common sense. Is it because they
haven't come to know You yet? They haven't come alive in
Your Spirit? Is that it?

Today's verse says that it's the spirit in a person that gives
true understanding. All the more reason why I need to let
them know about the kind of life they can experience in You,
Lord! Thank You, Jesus, for the peace that comes when Your
Spirit moves. Amen.

Sin Has No Dominion over Me!

For sin will have no dominion over you,
since you are not under law but under grace.

ROMANS 6:14 ESV

Sin is not my owner, Jesus. I used to think it was. I used to feel trapped with no way of escape from it. Sin ruled my life in many shapes and forms, and I couldn't figure out how to pull off the shackles that held me bound.

But You, Lord? You set me free from sin and death. Those things can't trap me any longer. I am not worried about the "do this, don't do that" stuff. I don't have to beat myself up whenever I mess up. I don't have to feel like there's no escape.

With You, there is always an escape! You offer grace, the perfect alternative to the tongue-lashing some would give. Hey, I've been pretty good at beating myself up at times too!

My heart is set free under Your amazing grace, Lord. Sin has no place in my life and will certainly not control me any longer. Thank You for that revelation! Amen.

As Clear as the Noonday Sun!

Let the Lord lead you and trust him to help. Then it will
be as clear as the noonday sun that you were right.

PSALM 37:5-6 CEV

Sometimes I catch a few minutes of the evening news, and I get so upset! Knowing what's going on out there robs me of my peace. There is so much injustice in this world. There are so many wrongs that need to be righted. So many false accusations and bold-faced lies coming over the airwaves, even from those we thought we could trust. It seems completely unfair, Jesus!

If I think about it too long, I get worked up. . .and not just for a few minutes. I lose my cool thinking about the way the world is. But You tell me to commit my way to You—to trust in You—and You will act. You will make things right.

I'm so glad that I can put my trust in You and not the wisdom of man. Eternal justice will prevail. I don't know when, but I do know how. You, Lord, will bring it to pass. And it will be an awesome thing when it happens! Help me hold my tongue until then, please! Amen.

Number Our Days

Teach us to number our days,
that we may gain a heart of wisdom.

PSALM 90:12 NIV

You created man to live forever, didn't You, Jesus? You never meant for us to die. Sometimes I think about what life would be like right now if Adam and Eve hadn't sinned. Would I exist? Would I live in the garden with them? Would that slippery snake still be messing with us?

When I look at verses like this one from Psalm 90, I'm reminded that Your whole plan all along wasn't for a short life here on earth, but for a blissful existence with You, our Creator. If Adam and Eve had never sinned, that beautiful garden would be ours for the taking! Nothing but perfection would greet us each morning.

Speaking of perfection, I realize we're headed to heaven soon. There, in the true Garden of Eden, all will be made known. Until then, I hope I never forget just how short this life is and how much You want us to spend every moment with You. I can't wait to spend forever with You, Jesus! Amen.

A Pursuer of Peace

Turn away from evil and do good;
seek peace and pursue it.

PSALM 34:14 ESV

Is it hiding under a bushel? Is it hidden away in a cabinet? Will I find it if I search under every rock or in every cobweb-filled corner? Your Word says that I can search for peace, and I will find it. If I pursue peace as a lifestyle, it will be mine for the taking. But I have to search it out. I can't assume that it's just going to appear unless I pursue You above all, Lord. I've also got to do my best to turn away from evil, like today's verse says. If I keep on sinning, I will never find peace. It will escape me all the days of my life. (I can't have my cake and eat it too! I can live in sin, or I can live in peace, but not both at the same time. It's my choice.)

Today I choose to let go of evil intentions, desires, and cravings. I come into Your presence pursuing not just Your peace, not just Your hand, but Your heart, Lord. Thank You for making me a peace chaser! Amen.

A Guarded Heart

*And the peace of God, which surpasses all
understanding, will guard your hearts
and your minds in Christ Jesus.*

PHILIPPIANS 4:7 ESV

I can't imagine living in a home that had no doors, Lord. What would it be like, knowing that anyone could walk in whenever they wanted? (Scary! I'll keep my doors and my locks, thank you very much!) In many ways, that's what it's like when I don't allow You to guard my heart. Your Word says that Your beyond-understanding peace is the doorway. It's the guard that leads to my heart.

When I'm worked up all the time, I leave the door wide open for the enemy to come in and mess things up. And boy, does he! If there's one thing the devil knows how to do, it's create chaos and confusion.

You never planned for me to live that way. Your Word tells me to guard my heart and my mind, so that's what I will do. I want every day to be a guarded day. . .guarded by the peace that only comes from You. Amen.

You're a Wide-Awake God

He will not let your foot slip—he who watches
over you will not slumber; indeed, he who watches
over Israel will neither slumber nor sleep.

PSALM 121:3-4 NIV

You never fall asleep on the job, Lord! When I'm about to trip and fall, when I fear I'm about to go down for the last time, You are right there, wide awake, taking care of me. You're not going to let me crash and burn. You have a handle on everything, even when I don't!

It gives me peace to know You're not a God who snoozes. You don't even take little catnaps! You're wide awake to see all that's happening while I slumber, and You've already got a solution for the problems I face.

So I will trust You, God, even when the path ahead looks slippery. With one word You can keep me walking firm, keep me from taking an unnecessary tumble. Thanks for staying awake and watching over me, Lord! Amen.

Live at Peace with Others

Be friendly with everyone. Don't be proud and feel that you are smarter than others. Make friends with ordinary people. Don't mistreat someone who has mistreated you. But try to earn the respect of others, and do your best to live at peace with everyone.

ROMANS 12:16–18 CEV

Jesus, You've called me to live alongside people of every race, every color, and every religion. I represent You when I'm loving and gracious to all people, even those who choose not to follow You. (It's not easy, but You ask me to try!) You placed me where I am to show Your love, Your affection, and Your path toward peace to everyone I meet, including those I agree with and those I don't.

I don't always get it right, Jesus, but I'm trying to do what is honorable in Your sight when I meet with difficult people face-to-face. As much as it depends on me, Lord, I'm doing everything I can to live at peace with all people—and to share Your truth along the way. Amen.

Safe in You

I've put my trust in all kinds of things, Jesus. For instance, I've trusted people with my heart, people who only broke it and left me shattered. Talk about painful! I've trusted in money then ended up broke. I've trusted in relatives only to be let down. I've even trusted in the alarm system on our house, but it went off at random times!

Honestly? The only place I can put my trust, the only place I am truly safe, is with You. You've explained this so well in today's verse, Jesus: "Don't fall into the trap of being a coward—trust the Lord, and you will be safe." I don't want to fall into any traps! I don't want to be caught up in earthly relationships. Whenever I do that, my heart is twisted and manipulated into doing whatever people talk me into. There's no safety in that! No, I'll stick with You, Jesus. It brings me great peace to know that You've got me covered. Amen.

Faithful in Much

"He that is faithful with little things is faithful with big things also. He that is not honest with little things is not honest with big things. If you have not been faithful with riches of this world, who will trust you with true riches? If you have not been faithful in that which belongs to another person, who will give you things to have as your own?"

LUKE 16:10-12 NLV

I'll admit it, Lord. Sometimes I don't take care of things like I should. My room gets messy. My homework doesn't get finished. The little things don't get done. Oops! (These things can become habits, I know!)

Oh, I've got plenty of excuses. I'm pretty busy, after all. But Your Word says that if I'm faithful in the little things, then You will give me bigger things. Maybe that's why some of my prayers haven't been answered yet. Are You waiting on me to prove that I can be faithful with what You've already given me, Lord?

Guide me to the areas of my life that need fixing, I pray. You will bring true peace when I get this right. Amen.

The Desire of My Heart

*May he give you the desire of your heart
and make all your plans succeed.*

PSALM 20:4 NIV

I'm a planner, Lord! Sometimes I map things out to the point of obsession. (Can we say control freak?) But, in spite of my over-the-top planning, nothing I've ever planned for my own life or the lives of those around me could come close to the plans that You have created for us, Your kids.

Your plans are for my hope. They are for my future. You want to give me the desires of my heart, and that brings me such joy! You're putting the pieces in place even now so that I can be successful in the things You've called me to do. You must see potential in me, which really boosts my confidence, not in myself but in You!

So, as I watch those plans come together, may I always have the assurance, the peace, that everything is working together for my good because of Your great love for me.

How grateful I am! Amen.

Nothing I've Done

For it is by grace you have been saved, through faith—and this is not from yourselves, it is the gift of God—not by works, so that no one can boast.

EPHESIANS 2:8–9 NIV

I've been known to brag on myself a time or two, Jesus. (Just keeping it real!) I perform some sort of feat, and I feel pretty good about myself. I start to think I'm all that and a bag of chips. After giving myself a few pats on the back, I share what I've done with others, doing my best to sound humble as I brag about my accomplishment.

Maybe I will accomplish some good things in my lifetime, Lord. But Your Word tells me that nothing I'll ever do will come close to the free gift of salvation that You gave me. Everything I do pales in comparison. Salvation is such an amazing gift, and You gave it at such a high cost! Eternal life is mine because of a Savior who allowed Himself to be nailed to a cross and crucified for my sins. I'm so grateful for the peace You bring through Your work on the cross, Jesus. You and only You! Amen.

I Trust Only in You

Some trust in chariots and some in horses,
but we trust in the name of the LORD our God.

PSALM 20:7 ESV

Some people put their trust in their grades. They think they're all that because of how smart they are! Others put their trust in a great-paying job. They think they can buy cool things if their paycheck is big enough. Others trust in fancy cars or expensive clothes. They have an image to maintain, after all. But me? I won't trust in anything but the name of the Lord my God.

In the name of Jesus, giants are defeated. Mountains have to move. They crumble with just the whisper of Your name, Jesus. Wow! It's in Your great name that I find safety and salvation. It's in Your great name that I overcome my struggles. And it's in Your great name, Jesus, that I have victory, no matter what I'm walking through.

I can't wait for the day when all Christians are gathered around Your throne crying out that amazing name: Jesus! Amen.

Because of What You Did

Now that we have been made right with
God by putting our trust in Him, we have
peace with Him. It is because of what
our Lord Jesus Christ did for us.

ROMANS 5:1 NLV

Some search for peace inside themselves. Others look for it in their image or other stuff they think is important. Some look for peace in the things that money can buy. Others look for peace in boyfriends or friendships.

But me? I've learned that peace only comes from one place, and that's a relationship with You. My peace cost You a lot, Jesus! If it hadn't been for Your death on the cross, I would never have been saved! If I hadn't been saved, I wouldn't have peace with You. Peace can only come through You, my Lord Jesus Christ.

You came, You died, You were buried, and You rose again. (Wow!) Because of all that, I now have peace. I can never thank You enough, Jesus! You did it all for me. Amen.

No Weapon Formed

"No weapon that is fashioned against you shall succeed, and you shall refute every tongue that rises against you in judgment. This is the heritage of the servants of the LORD and their vindication from me, declares the LORD."

ISAIAH 54:17 ESV

It's hard to imagine the people I love using weapons against me, but it happens! When I find out that someone I care about has gone behind my back to lie about me, to hurt me, to falsely accuse me, it's always such a shock. It's the last thing I expect! I would like to be able to trust those around me. But many of them are tricky, whether I see it or not. Some have twisted thinking. (They're listening to the enemy, that slippery devil!) Really, *all* human beings are capable of hurting others.

This is why I love today's verse so much, Jesus! It promises me that no weapon made to be used against me can prosper. No devious plans. No gossip. No lies. No heartbreak. With You on my side, no enemy can succeed, no matter how hard he tries. You will win that battle every single time. I'm so grateful! Amen.

Pleasing to You, Lord

Sin has been paid for by loving-kindness and truth.
The fear of the Lord keeps one away from sin. When
the ways of a man are pleasing to the Lord, He makes
even those who hate him to be at peace with him.

PROVERBS 16:6-7 NLV

I want to live in a way that brings joy to Your heart, Jesus! I want to make You happy, not just with my actions but with my attitude. You're teaching me that when I live like that, when I genuinely try to please You, others pay attention. They see all the cool changes in my life, then they want what I have.

This is even true of my enemies, Lord! They see my calm reactions and decide to lay down their swords. When I'm at peace, they begin to desire peace too. (It's contagious!) I want to be a real reflection of You—not to show off but so others will come to know You. May I always live a life that's pleasing to You, Jesus! Amen.

You Won't Deny Yourself

If we are faithless, he remains faithful—
for he cannot deny himself.

2 TIMOTHY 2:13 ESV

We were created in Your image to do good things, Jesus. When we hurt others, it breaks Your heart. No wonder! We're not acting like You at all, are we? It's not really in our born-again nature to bring harm to others or to inflict pain. We were born again to bring life! And yet, we still mess up from time to time.

But You? One thing I'm learning about You, Jesus, is You don't go against Your nature. Ever. You simply can't. You won't deny Yourself in that way.

Even if I am faithless, God, You are still faithful because it is always in Your nature to be so. Even when I'm unloving, You never are. You couldn't be. I want to fully have Your nature! I want to live in a way that brings healing and peace to everyone I meet. Help me. . .please.

And Lord? Thanks for the peace that comes with knowing You are never unfaithful to Yourself or to me. Amen.

I Lay Them at Your Feet

Do not worry. Learn to pray about everything. Give thanks to God as you ask Him for what you need. The peace of God is much greater than the human mind can understand. This peace will keep your hearts and minds through Christ Jesus.

PHILIPPIANS 4:6–7 NLV

I'm pretty needy, Jesus. I'm always knocking on Your door, asking for this or that. I'm usually hoping You'll grant my every wish, like a genie in a bottle.

Sometimes I get pretty worked up, hoping You will do what I ask (okay, demand). But Your Word reminds me that if I want to have peace, if I want to be rid of anxiety, I should be anxious for nothing. (This is harder than it sounds, Lord!) You want me to come to You with genuine prayers, asking for Your perfect will for my life. Then You will pour out Your great peace. You'll guard my heart and my mind.

Here I come! I'm headed in Your direction, Lord, ready to do it Your way. Thanks for the reminder that I can live above these circumstances that are in front of me. Amen.

You Bring Healing

Christ carried the burden of our sins. He was nailed to the cross, so that we would stop sinning and start living right. By his cuts and bruises you are healed.

1 PETER 2:24 CEV

I think about this sometimes, Jesus: If You had not given Your life, if there had been no cross, would I have ever found healing in my heart? In my emotions? In my relationships? Without the cross, healing would just be a dream, a fantasy—something to wish for but never to achieve. How sad I would be without Your path to freedom, Father!

Thank You, Jesus, for the cross! Thank You for taking the stripes on Your back so that I could have wholeness and healing and peace. What a heavy price You paid for it all, my Savior! I'm humbled by the cross. I'm broken by the cross. I'm healed by the cross. And I can never express my gratitude enough, but I will do my best to try to thank You for all that took place that awful, wonderful day when my sins were washed away! Amen.

The Ancient Paths

This is what the L<small>ORD</small> says: "Stand at the crossroads and look; ask for the ancient paths, ask where the good way is, and walk in it, and you will find rest for your souls. But you said, 'We will not walk in it.'"

JEREMIAH 6:16 NIV

Sometimes I feel stuck and don't know which way to go, Jesus. But Your Word shows me examples to help guide me. There are amazing stories I can learn from. There are great men and women from the Old and New Testaments who can teach me a thing or two if I'm really paying attention.

I learn from Abraham, Isaac, and Jacob. I get truth from the Proverbs 31 woman and from heroes like Hannah and Deborah. I see how to share my faith when I study the lives of Peter, Paul, Timothy, and Silas.

So, when I'm feeling stuck, when I'm not sure which way to go, I will look to the men and women of old who walked with You. I will learn from their mistakes, and I will grow from the things they did correctly. And I will step boldly into whatever plan You have for my life, Lord, so that I can make a difference in the world like they did. Amen.

A Pure Heart

*Create in me a pure heart, O God,
and renew a steadfast spirit within me.*

PSALM 51:10 NIV

You are the great Creator, Jesus! Everything that was ever made was formed by You. I might consider myself to be creative, but I'm really just taking what You've already given me and changing it up a bit. People might claim to invent, but they're just building on what You started. You've given us a great foundation.

Of all Your creative work, probably the most amazing is the miracle You've done in my heart. It's more colorful than any rainbow, more active than any volcano, and more breathtaking than any mountain peak.

You create and re-create—and all for my benefit and Your glory. I stand in awe of You, Lord! And to think, You can take this heart, even on the hardest day, and wash it clean, making all things fresh and new. What an awesome God You are! Amen.

Not by Human Wisdom

When I talked with you or preached, I didn't
try to prove anything by sounding wise.
I simply let God's Spirit show his power.
That way you would have faith because of God's
power and not because of human wisdom.

1 CORINTHIANS 2:4–5 CEV

If I went to college for a zillion years and got lots of degrees, it wouldn't make me wise in Your sight, Jesus. Hey, I'm not saying I have something against education, but I'm definitely learning that answers are not found in human wisdom.

The Bible says the Holy Spirit's power will show me where true wisdom is. So today I draw close to You and invite Your Spirit to bring changes to my heart and mind. Afterward, I'll take what I've learned to others. They'll see the changes in me and want what I have!

When I see You working in the lives of my friends and family, I get so excited! You have big plans for all of us. Thank You for the education You give. Amen.

Still Waters

The LORD is my shepherd, I lack nothing.
He makes me lie down in green pastures,
he leads me beside quiet waters.

PSALM 23:1-2 NIV

Your Word says that You lead me beside quiet waters, Jesus. I stare at them, noticing how quiet and still they are, and I think, *Wow! God must wish my life looked like this. . .peaceful and still.* Only, it doesn't. Things are kind of a mess!

It's not easy, figuring out how to calm things down. . .until I come to You, Jesus. There, in Your presence, my heart starts beating a little slower. The worrying stops. The confusion ends. I can see—without the chaos swirling around me—that things might actually calm down, right there, in the middle of the storm. Thank You for leading me beside still waters so that I can be reminded of the peaceful heart You're working so hard to create inside of me. Amen.

You've Been Planning This Awhile!

You, LORD, are my God! I will praise you for doing the wonderful things you had planned and promised since ancient times.

ISAIAH 25:1 CEV

When I'm planning for a big trip, sometimes I start getting ready months ahead of time. Hey, I can't help myself! You see how excited I am, Jesus! I want to see those plane tickets. I want to make sure Mom has booked the hotel. I even start to map out what the days will look like. A good plan gets me excited about the adventure. (Then again, I'm already adventurous!)

Your plans for my life were carefully thought out too. Long before I ever existed, You started thinking of me, didn't You, Lord? You put a l-o-t more care into preparing for my journey than I ever could for any vacation or trip. Thanks for getting all the little details ironed out, Lord. You take such great care with the road You've prepared for me. I'm super grateful! Amen.

Your Plans Stand Forever!

But the plans of the LORD stand firm forever,
the purposes of his heart through all generations.

PSALM 33:11 NIV

Your plans stand forever, Jesus. What an amazing promise from today's verse! The work You're doing in me? It's going to pass from me to my kids. . .and even to their kids. It can travel across generations!

You never change, so I can count on You to stay the same, no matter what. When everything around me is shaking, You are as steady as a rock. Your plans are not built on shifting sand. Whew! That's good news!

Why do I know I can trust You? What brings such peace to my heart? You and only You, Jesus. I'm so glad Your plans don't crumble. They don't shake. They don't fade away over time. Instead, they stand forever. . .and ever. . .and ever. Amen.

I Trust My Life to You

Each morning let me learn more about your love because I trust you. I come to you in prayer, asking for your guidance.

PSALM 143:8 CEV

Show me what to do, Jesus. When You give directions, I will follow. Every morning is like a fresh start, a chance to witness Your love. You guide me with it! It's easy to submit to You because of Your great love.

I know I can trust You. You've given me no reason not to! In fact, You've proven many times over that I'm always on Your mind. (Have I mentioned I'm grateful for that?) So I will follow Your unfailing love, which guides me, gives me courage, and floods my heart with peace. As I head down the road on my journey with You, I will have everything I could need and more.

Lead me. Guide me. Take me down the path that will make my relationship with You even stronger, I pray. I trust my life to You, Lord! Amen.

How Vast the Sum!

How precious to me are your thoughts,
God! How vast is the sum of them!

PSALM 139:17 NIV

Not everyone is great at math, Jesus. Adding things? It sure is easier with a calculator. But there's one thing I don't need a calculator for. When I look around at Your great plans, Your thoughts for my life and for the people I love, they are far too great to count. There's no adding machine that can tally them up.

How great is Your love for mankind! How vast, how huge, are Your blessings. You were always thinking of us, even when You spun the earth into existence and placed man on it. You were thinking of us at the cross when the ultimate sacrifice took place. And You were thinking of us as You pushed back that stone and stepped out of the grave.

We were—and are always—on Your mind, Lord. I'm humbled by that truth. Truly humbled. I pray You're on my mind just as much. Amen.

Your Holy House

Happy is the man You choose and bring near to You to live in Your holy place. We will be filled with the good things of Your house, Your holy house.

PSALM 65:4 NLV

I love this verse so much, Jesus! It's a promise from Your Word that I'll be happy in Your house. When I choose to live with You, to hang out with You every day, You say, *"Watch this! You're gonna love it here!"*

This is one reason it's so cool to draw close to You. I don't come for what You can give me, but that doesn't stop You from pouring out blessings! In fact, You do everything You can to delight me when I show up and spend one-on-one time with You. There in that precious, holy place, You give me peace, joy, love, faith, mercy. . .and so much more. Your blessings make my (already fabulous!) life even better.

I'm learning, Jesus! You are a "pour it out" Savior! I want to live inside the safety of Your holy courts forever. I will meet You there. Amen.

My Thinking. . .Transformed!

Don't copy the behavior and customs of this world, but let God transform you into a new person by changing the way you think. Then you will learn to know God's will for you, which is good and pleasing and perfect.

ROMANS 12:2 NLT

Sometimes I get so caught up in what's trending—whether it's fashion, hairdos, or decorating ideas for my bedroom. I want to be like the cool kids, keeping up with the times. I've seen this in the church too, people copying the behaviors of the world. Some even pretend to be holy at church, but their actions outside the church walls make them appear anything but!

But Lord, You don't want me to follow others. You want to transform me into a brand-new person. This includes the way I think. If I allow this process—and sometimes it is a process—then I can have total peace of mind. Whew! That sounds really good right now.

When my mind is peaceful, Lord, I can discover Your perfect will for me. I want to know all that You have planned for me! I'm sure it's going to be amazing! So transform me today, I pray. Amen.

Return, My Soul

Return to your rest, my soul,
for the LORD has been good to you.

PSALM 116:7 NIV

I have to admit that I'm addicted to certain foods, Jesus. Some are good for me, but others are definitely not. Still, they're my go-to. I return to them again and again. I would be embarrassed if people saw me scarfing them down.

Today You are calling me to a different sort of addiction. You want me to return to the rest I once experienced with You. You're drawing me to a peaceful, quiet existence with my Creator, the Lover of my soul. You're drawing me in with Your love, saying, *"Come to Me, and I will refresh you and make you whole again."* I want to crave this rest in the same way I long for that candy bar or ice cream, Lord! I want to be drawn back to You, back to the peace and rest that only You can bring.

You've been so good to me. How could I doubt that Your rest would ever bring me anything but delight? So I return— to You! Amen.

A Stronghold in the Day of Trouble

The Lord is good, a strong refuge when trouble comes.
He is close to those who trust in him.

NAHUM 1:7 NLT

You never promised me a trouble-free life, Lord. In fact, Your Word says that there will be a lot of big troubles in this life; but it also says that I shouldn't let them get me down because You overcame the world. (What a relief, to know I'm not the only one going through hard times! We all face troubles, Lord, but You're aware. . .and You're there.)

I won't be surprised when troubles come my way. I won't get down in the dumps, thinking that You have abandoned me. I know better. And I will continue to wait for that moment when You show up and show off! (You're pretty amazing like that!)

You are my hiding place when trouble comes. That's all I need to remember when I'm starting to panic. You're close to me when I place my trust in You—You're never more than a prayer away. Thank You for being my safe place in the day of trouble, Lord! Amen.

You Went Around Doing Good

"And you know that God anointed Jesus of Nazareth with the Holy Spirit and with power. Then Jesus went around doing good and healing all who were oppressed by the devil, for God was with him."

ACTS 10:38 NLT

I can learn how to live a holy life by watching You, Jesus! The Bible says that You went around doing good. (That's step one! Be good to people.)

You had the power of the Holy Spirit, Jesus. You moved in power everywhere You went, performing awesome miracles. I want to move forward in power too. Wow, if only I had the ability to witness miracles!

Oh, wait. . .I do! You said You will work through me, Lord. Lead me to those who need prayer—the hurting, the lost, the broken. Lead me to the ones who've given up hope, so that I can reach out and touch them with Your power and with words of love. I want to be a blessing to everyone I come in contact with, not so people will see me as holy but because I love them. Give me Your passion and Your compassion for others, I pray. I want to be like Jesus. Amen.

I Stand in Awe of You!

The fear of the Lord leads to life, and he who has it will sleep well, and will not be touched by sin.

PROVERBS 19:23 NLV

Jesus, when I was younger, I didn't understand what it meant to fear You. I thought maybe You were telling me that I should be terrified of You, that my knees should knock and my hands should tremble if I dared get close to You or ask You for anything.

I've figured it out now! You want me to stand in awe of You, to recognize that You are 100 percent holy and perfect. Mary Poppins might have thought that she was "practically perfect in every way," but only You are perfect, Jesus. No one else. So I come to You with holy fear, overwhelmed by Your glory!

I have no reason to be afraid of You. When I stand in awe of You, when I fully understand Your authority in my life, then I'm completely peaceful. Thank You for showing me Your holiness, Lord. Amen.

Higher

"For as the heavens are higher than the earth, so are my ways higher than your ways and my thoughts than your thoughts."

ISAIAH 55:9 ESV

I like the way You think, Jesus! Your thoughts are w-a-y higher than mine. I can't imagine how You dream up so many cool things. Your thoughts are too marvelous for me to even pretend to understand. You're ten million times smarter than any college professor!

Today's verse says that the heavens are higher than the earth. I sometimes wonder what heaven will be like. I'll probably stand there completely silent as I take it all in for the first time. I'm guessing the dazzling beauty will take my breath away!

One thing is for sure—You are greater, Lord. Your ways are greater. Your imagination is greater. Your thoughts are greater. Your design is greater. And because of all that, my peace can be greater. I've put my trust in the One who dreamed up sunrises and sunsets, rainbows and tadpoles. I praise You, my great Creator! Amen.

A Willing Spirit

Let the joy of Your saving power return to me.
And give me a willing spirit to obey you.

PSALM 51:12 NLV

I'll admit it, Jesus—sometimes You have to drag me kicking and screaming to the place where You want me to go. I don't follow willingly. I make it hard on You. (Sorry about that.) I can be a slow learner at times and a bit stubborn too. (Can we blame it on my personality? No? I didn't think so.)

Today, Lord, I give You a willing spirit. I want to obey the first time You ask. I won't make You drag me there. I won't be that rebellious child stomping my foot and insisting we do things my way. I'm learning that Your way is truly better. You've got great things planned for me, so why would I fight the process? (I know, I know. . .you would think I would have learned this before now.) Here I am, Jesus! No kicking and screaming today, I promise. Amen.

Unity of Mind

*Last of all, you must share the same thoughts
and the same feelings. Love each other with a
kind heart and with a mind that has no pride.*

1 PETER 3:8 NLV

Walking in unity sounds easy enough until the teacher asks me to work on a group project. Then my peace flies out the window, Jesus! There are w-a-y too many different personalities in the group, and everyone has a different idea about how we should move forward. Ugh! Things can get heated, especially if there are rude people in the group.

But You have called us to be united, like-minded, kind toward each other, loving each other regardless of our differences, with no pride. (You almost lost me at "no pride," Lord. That's a tough one when I'm dealing with cranky, demanding people!)

I'm learning that living at peace with hard people is impossible unless I give the situation to You. If I want to be at peace with those around me, I must live the way You say...and You're all about unity, Lord. Oh boy, am I ever going to need Your help with this one! Amen.

You Choose Not to Remember, Lord!

Do not remember the rebellious sins of my youth. Remember me in the light of your unfailing love, for you are merciful, O LORD.

PSALM 25:7 NLT

Jesus, I'm so grateful You're not keeping a record of all my wrongs! When I think back to some of the things I did as a kid. . .oh boy. You not keeping a tally is great news for me because mine would be sooo long. You don't have a naughty list with my name on it.

You're a forgiving, gracious God. I'll never understand how or why You love me like You do or why You chose to cover my sins without asking me to pay the price, but I'm eternally (yes, eternally) grateful!

May I be as forgiving and gracious to others as You have been to me. If You can choose not to remember, maybe I can too. I promise to try! It gives me great peace to know that You're not holding my sins against me. Amen.

I Will See Your Goodness

I remain confident of this: I will see the goodness
of the LORD in the land of the living.

PSALM 27:13 NIV

You provide everything we need, Jesus! There's food in our pantry, water pouring from our faucet, and electricity to turn on the lights. There's gas in my parents' car, money in the bank (a little!), and clothing in my closet. You've taken such great care of us, and we are all so thankful!

I won't take these special gifts for granted. The way You provide is a gift. Show us how to appreciate it all and never forget where it comes from. You've always been there, taking care of us, and that gives me such peace! If You take care of the birds, giving them seed to eat, then I know You've got me covered, not just now but as I grow up, graduate from high school, and go on to whatever You have next for me.

I will remain confident in this: that I will go on seeing Your goodness, Lord. You've proven it time and time again, after all. I can live at peace knowing that You will provide for me the rest of my days. Amen.